Seven End-Times Messages From God

Copyright 2009
Rev. Edward G. Palmer
All Rights Reserved

Seven End-Times Messages From God

Seven End-Times Messages From God

Copyright © 2009 by Edward G. Palmer
Published by JVED Publishing
Elk River, Minnesota 55330

ISBN 978-0-9768833-7-1 (Seven End-Times Messages From God)

Palmer, Edward G.
    1. Faith—The Apostle Edward
    2. Bible Prophecy—The End-Times
    3. Christianity—Trinity Doctrine

Printed in the United States of America.

All rights reserved. No portion of this book may be reproduced in any form without the written permission of the Author.

Thank you for purchasing "Seven End-Times Messages From God." Copyright laws protect this written work of Reverend Edward G. Palmer. Distribution to others in any form is a violation of copyright laws. Volume discounts are available. Contact the author for further details. Thank you for respecting copyright laws. God will bless your honesty. This work is a ministry to Christians with God's message that they need to love HIS Word more than they love the doctrines of their Church.

Notice. This book and its entire contents represents the sole opinion of Reverend Edward G. Palmer based upon his thirty plus years of in-depth Bible studies, his actual life experiences, his personal diaries and publicly available documents including religious ecumenical documents. No part of this book is intended to offer professional counseling of any type. Persons involved in cultic churches, those in need of spiritual counseling, religious or any other professional advice should seek competent professional help.

Capitalization Protocol. On all Bible citations, regardless of the translation used, and where the context clearly points to God Almighty or to Jesus Christ, this book makes the distinction between the two by using either small cap characters or lower case characters. For God Almighty, a small capitalized style protocol is followed and reflected in the format: CREATOR, FATHER, GIVER, HE, HIS, HIM, HIMSELF, YOU, YOUR, ME, MINE, MOST HIGH, MY, MYSELF, LORD and SAVIOR, ETC. For Jesus Christ, a lower case protocol is used except for Lord and Son. Hence, when these pronouns are used for Jesus, they show up as: he, his, him, himself, you, your, me, my, myself, savior, Lord, or Son. This has generally been followed throughout the book, but is not the case with every cited verse. It is used for those verses in which the context cannot be easily disputed or in the case of citing a quality or attribute, which belongs solely to God. For those interested in the original translation capitalization, the author refers them to the actual Bible version used for the cited text. A list of Bible translations is shown on the next page. In some other cases, capital letters used within the cited sentence structure were also changed on common words for ease of reading or modern grammar. In other cases, the capitalized letters were left as shown in the original translation. Hence the original Bible phrase "; Because" might appear as "; because." In all instances, Apostle Edward maintains complete integrity of translation and the writings herein can be traced back to the original Bibles to confirm the accuracy of presentation. While not perfect, the capitalization protocol is fairly consistent and enhances the reading and value of Apostle Edward's teachings.

Translation Notice & Bible Definitions

The following Bible translations were researched for this book along with three Hebrew texts and one or more ancient manuscripts such as the Book of Enoch (ENO). Except where otherwise indicated and in regards to capitalization of words, all Scripture quotations are taken from the Holy Bible, New King James Version © 1979, 1980, 1982 by Thomas Nelson, Inc., Publishers. Verses that are followed by a two, three or four-letter capitalized identifier are from the following Bible translations or reference works.

Abbreviation	Bible Definition
KJV	King James Version [1]
AMP	Amplified Bible [3]
ASB	American Standard [4]
BBE	Bible In Basic English [7]
CEV	Contemporary English Version [8]
DB	Darby Bible [9]
DR	Douay-Rheims 1957 Catholic Bible [10]
ENO	Book of Enoch - Richard Laurence 1883 Ed [11]
ESV	English Standard Version [12]
GEN	Geneva Bible [13]
GN	Good News [14] -Today's English Bible
GNA	Good News Apocrypha [15]
GW	God's Word Bible [16]
HEB	Hebrew Bible — English JPS 1917 Edition [17]
HOL	Holman Christian Standard Bible [18]
ICB	International Children's Bible [19]
JSB	Jewish Study Bible [20] - JPS 1985, 1999
LIV	Living Bible [21]
MB	MicroBible [23]
MES	The Message [24]
MLT	Morris Literal Translation [25]
MOF	James Moffatt Translation, Final Edition [26]

Bible Definitions (Continued)

Abbreviation	Bible Definition
NAB	New American Bible 1991 - Catholic Bible [27]
NASB	New American Standard Bible [5]; +1977 Ed [6]
NET	New English Translation [28]
NIV	New International Version [29]
NCV	New Century Version [30]
NJB	New Jerusalem Bible [31]
NKJV	New King James Version [2]
NLT	New Living Translation [22]
NRSV	New Revised Standard Version [35]
PNT	Phillips New Testament Bible [32]
REB	Revised English Bible [33]
RSV	Revised Standard Version [34]
SET	Simple English Translation [36]
TAN	Tanach - The Stone Edition 1996 [37]
TB	Transliterated Bible [38]
WEB	Webster's Bible [39]
WES	Wesley New Testament [40]
WEY	Weymouth's NT [41]
YLT	Young's Literal Translation [42]

Contents

Introduction

Copyright Notice i
Capitalization Protocol ii
Translation Notice & Bible Definitions .... iii-iv
Table of Contents v
Foreword .... vi-ix

The End-Times 1-37

Seven Messages From God

The Invitation 39-58
The Messenger 61-75
The Message 77-97
Law of Christ 99-119
The Seven Spirits 121-138
The Tithe Lie 141-159
The Unfaithful 161-178

Appendixes

A - A Real Salvation Prayer 181-184
B - Baptism Doctrine 185-188
C - Thomas' Exclamation 189-192
Notes 193-197
Scripture Cross Reference 199-205
Apostle Edward asks, "Are you ready?" 207-208
Free Newsletter & Contact Information 209-215

Foreword

God gave me the *Seven Messages* beginning in December of 2007 and during 2008 they were finished. I had thought that these were to be used mainly as streets tracts to help Christians understand who God is and who His only human begotten Son, Jesus Christ is. Yet, God has asked me to put them into this book form for you.

Most Christians believe that Jesus is God and worship him as such. Yet to do so commits idolatry in God's eyes and totally misses the essence of the message He gave Jesus to tell us. This is just one of the myths in these End-Times. A more complete picture of the many myths present in Christianity can be found in the *Book of Edward: Christian Mythology*. This is a four-volume book set that explains who Jesus is talking to when he said: "I never knew you" in Matthew 7:21-23. Of course, he was talking to Christians who thought that they were saved. They weren't and he rejected them.

You will find out why in the *Book of Edward* available from all bookstores and also online at http://www.bookofedward.org.

It is not the intent of this book to fully explain the trinity doctrine that was created in 325 AD at the First Ecumenical Council of Nicea. If you want to understand the trinity doctrine further, please see my book titled *Trinity Dogma*. You will find it available from all bookstores and online at http://www.trinitydogma.com.

I had presented the *Seven Messages* to a few Christians and was amazed at how little impact God's Word had on them regarding the false trinity doctrine and the identity of God. *Trinity Dogma* was written to help Christians understand the identity of God from God's own words found in their own version of His Holy Bible.

Jesus actually identifies God in John 20:17. The apostle Paul then confirms God's identify in 1 Corinthians 8:6. To claim that Jesus is God literally makes Jesus a liar. It also makes Paul a liar.

All bibles have Jesus and Paul identifying the FATHER as our only God. This is to say that all bibles have John 20:17 and 1 Corinthians 8:6 stating the very same thing. God is clearly and unambiguously identified in the New Testament. It is the same God of the Old Testament. It is the God of the Jews; the God that Jesus worshipped and called us to worship "in spirit and truth." Yet how can you do that if you do not even know who God truly is?

Each one of the seven messages is available in the form of a street tract for non-profit publication and distribution by ministries that seek to impart these End-Times messages. This is important so people can learn the true identity of God and the role Jesus played. If you represent a ministry that wants to distribute one or more of these seven messages as a street tract write to me for additional information. My contact information is at the back of this book.

I would also like to hear from you if this book has touched your life in any positive way, especially if it has motivated you to study God's Word or has helped you understand God's true identity.

If your faith is solely in the church you attend, this book may have a very negative impact upon your spiritual life. However, if your faith is grounded in our God and HIS Word, your soul will rejoice having read this book.

It took me 50 years before I fully understood the truth of God's Word. I spent four years in a Christian cult observing apostasy for God. Then, HE took me out of the organized doctrinal church to deprogram me with HIS Word. Virtually every orthodox Christian has been programmed with lies about the nature of God and HIS Son, Jesus Christ. It's now time to rejoice having found HIS truth.

> **Jesus said, "Whoever belongs to God <u>hears the words of God</u>; for this reason you do not listen, because you do not belong to God."**
> **John 8:47 (NAB)**

Do you hear the "words of God?"

That is what I offer to you in this book. I offer God's words, not my interpretation of HIS words. However, I cannot get you or anyone else to "listen." In fact, it's not even my job. That is a job for God's Spirit of Truth also known as the Holy Spirit. Pray!

It's not only God's words that you need to listen to. You also need to listen to the words of HIS only begotten human Son, Jesus.

> **God said, "This is my beloved Son, with whom I am well pleased; <u>listen to him</u>."**
> **Matthew 17:5 (NAB)**

This isn't very complicated. It is a matter of simply listening to God's Word and the teachings of Jesus Christ. You'll find out soon that Jesus only provided us with what God told him to say. Ergo, if you listen to Jesus, you are listening to a prophet with instructions from God for our benefit and consumption.

Yet, if you let church doctrines take a higher priority over the actual written word of God, you will not listen to God and HIS instructions will be lost on you. If you do not listen to Jesus, the same thing applies. God's instructions for your life will be lost.

Do you "listen to Jesus?"

So, the main challenge you will face with this book is to reconcile God's words, viewable from within your own Holy Bible, with the teachings of your church, which you have been taught as the truth. You will soon find out that Church teachings and the actual written words of God and the teachings of Jesus are different. So, who is telling you the truth about God? Who should you believe? Choose to believe our Lord Jesus Christ. He told us the truth about God!

Apostle Edward

The End-Times

> "Now as [Jesus] sat on the Mount of Olives, the disciples came to him privately, saying, 'Tell us, when will these things be? And what will be the sign of your coming, and of the end of the age?' " Matthew 24:3

Can We Actually Be In Biblical End-Times?

Jesus continues the discussion with his disciples on the Mount of Olives in Matthew 24-25 and tells them the following facts about the end of the age. Ergo, Jesus teaches us about the End-Times.

Matthew 24

"And Jesus answered and said to them: Take heed that no one <u>deceives</u> you. [5] For many will come in my name, saying, 'I am the Christ,' and will deceive many. [6] And you will hear of wars and rumors of wars. See that you are not troubled; for all these things must come to pass, but the end is not yet. [7] For nation will rise against nation, and kingdom against kingdom. And there will be famines, pestilences, and earthquakes in various places. [8] All these are the beginning of sorrows. [9] Then they will deliver you up to tribulation and kill you, and you will be hated by all nations for my name's sake. [10] And then many will be offended, will betray one another, and will hate one another. [11] Then many false prophets will rise up and deceive many. [12] And because lawlessness will abound, the love of many will grow cold. [13] But he who endures to the end shall be saved. [14] And this gospel of the kingdom will be preached in all the world as a witness to all the nations, and then the end will come."

[15] "Therefore when you see the 'abomination of desolation,' spoken of by Daniel the prophet, standing in the holy place (whoever reads, let him understand), [16] then let those who are in Judea flee to the mountains. [17] Let him who is on the housetop not go down to take anything out of his house. [18] And let him who is in the field not go back to get his clothes. [19] But woe to those who are pregnant and to those who are nursing babies in those days!"

[20] "And pray that your flight may not be in winter or on the Sabbath. [21] For then there will be great tribulation, such as has not been since the beginning of the world until this time, no, nor ever shall be. [22] And unless those days were shortened, no flesh would be saved; but for the elect's sake those days will be shortened. [23] Then if anyone says to you, 'Look, here is the Christ!' or 'There!' do not believe it. [24] For false Christs and false prophets will rise and show great signs and wonders to deceive, if possible, even the elect."

[25] "See, I have told you beforehand. [26] Therefore, if they say to you, 'Look, he [Christ] is in the desert!' do not go out; or 'Look, he [Christ] is in the inner rooms!' do not believe it. [27] For as the lightning comes from the east and flashes to the west, so also will the coming of the Son of Man be. [28] For wherever the carcass is, there the eagles will be gathered together."

[29] "Immediately after the tribulation of those days the sun will be darkened, and the moon will not give its light; the stars will fall from heaven, and the powers of the heavens will be shaken. [30] Then the sign of the Son of Man will appear in heaven, and then all the tribes of the earth will mourn, and they will see the Son of Man coming on the clouds of heaven with power and great glory. [31] And he will send HIS angels with a great sound of a trumpet, and they will gather together HIS elect from the four winds, from one end of heaven to the other."

[32] "Now learn this parable from the fig tree: When its branch has already become tender and puts forth leaves, you know that summer is near. [33] So you also, when you see all these things, know that it is near — at the doors! [34] Assuredly, I say to you, this generation will by no means pass away till all these things take place. [35] Heaven and earth will pass away, but MY [God's] words will by no means pass away."

[36] "But of that day and hour no one knows, not even the angels of heaven, but my FATHER only. [37] But as the days of Noah were, so also will the coming of the Son of Man be. [38] For as in the days before the flood, they were eating and drinking, marrying and giving in marriage, until the day that Noah entered the ark, [39] and did not know until the flood came and took them all away, so also will the coming of the Son of Man be. [40] Then two men will be in the field: one will be taken and the other left. [41] Two women will be grinding at the mill: one will be taken and the other left. [42] Watch therefore, for you do not know what hour your Lord is coming. [43] But know this, that if the master of the house had known what hour the thief would come, he would have watched and not allowed his house to be broken into. [44] Therefore you also be ready, for the Son of Man is coming at an hour you do not expect."

[45] "Who then is a faithful and wise servant, whom his master made ruler over his household, to give them food in due season? [46] Blessed is that servant whom his master, when he comes, will find so doing. [47] Assuredly, I say to you that he will make him ruler over all his goods. [48] But if that evil servant says in his heart, 'My master is delaying his coming,' [49] and begins to beat his fellow servants, and to eat and drink with the drunkards, [50] the master of that servant will come on a day when he is not looking for him and at an hour that he is not aware of, [51] and will cut him in two and appoint him his portion with the hypocrites. There shall be weeping and gnashing of teeth."

We learn from Jesus' teachings in Matthew 24 that certain End-Times events take place before the end of the age, as we know it in human terms. Are you ready? Do you see what I see? Can you hear the words of God? Are you listening to Jesus?

Jesus' End-Times Teachings In Matthew 24

What has already taken place or is currently happening and taking place before our very eyes are the following five listed events. Yet, Jesus did not just give us a list of events that have taken place or will take place in the future. Jesus also gives us a timeline, which points with accuracy to the exact place in "spiritual history" that we are now at. Jesus also foretells what will be coming. What is missing in Jesus' teaching is the time of future events. However, one thing is very clear, Scripture teaches we could recognize the season and it is clear that we are in the season of End-Time events.

Events Passed Or Now Happening

1. Deception

"Take heed that no one deceives you." V4-5

Deception in Christianity is rampant now. Many churches actually teach against God's Word. That includes all major denomination churches and those that are non-denominational. Most of them have an agenda and it is not to teach God's Word. This Church deception is documented in this book, the *Trinity Dogma* book and the four-volume *Book of Edward*, which God called me to write.

Jesus continues on with the words "Many will come in my name saying, 'I am the Christ.' " I first saw a large newspaper ad in the 1970's claiming Christ was then back on the earth and would come down in a few weeks from where he was. Prophecy fulfilled. Yet, today there is even a man in Florida who claims he is the Christ!

2. Wars and Rumors of Wars

"You will hear of wars and rumors of wars." V6

One would have to be dead not to observe all of the wars going on and the rumors of wars to come. The Iraq and Afghanistan wars are obvious examples of existing wars. The Islamic Jihad threat and the constant North Korean saber rattling are examples of war rumors. Yet, if you closely examine this issue, it would astound you as to the actual wars and conflicts going on globally.

3. Troubling and Gut Wrenching Times

"See that you are not troubled; for all these things must come to pass, but the end is not yet." V6

Jesus says these will be difficult times, which can literally scare many souls to death. If not scared to death, souls will be troubled with great anxiety, losing sleep and everything else that goes with high stress. YET, we are told, "Do not be troubled." How can we accomplish such a task? It is by understanding God's ways and accepting the "perfect peace that passes all human understanding," which we are offered through our faith in Jesus. There are two realities. One is sensed with our human abilities. The other is only sensed with our spiritual abilities. You cannot live in peace if you are focused on worldly events. You will only be tormented. To get peace, you must surrender to God. This starts by accepting Jesus Christ and praying the salvation prayers in this book.

It is possible to live within the eye of the earthly spiritual storm that is unfolding. There is calm at the center of hurricanes. God is the center of the coming spiritual storm. Seek peace and shelter under His spiritual wings and in the comfort of Jesus' teachings.

4. Nations Rising Against Nations

"Nation will rise against nation, and kingdom against kingdom." V7

Follow the news and you get a clear picture of this unfolding. Today there is a global economic crisis fueling a lot of this conflict, but the availability of oil for powering the economic engine of many countries is also part of it. It is no secret that China is rapidly building up its military and naval forces to protect its access to Mideast oil. Many believe it is a direct threat to the naval forces of the United States. We see pirates making a comeback in the coast off of Somalia. And, the global Jihad waged by Muslim extremists in Islam is a kingdom issue with no national boundaries.

5. Famines, Pestilences, Earthquakes

"There will be famines, pestilences, and earthquakes in various places." V7

Hardly a day goes by without the news talking about earthquakes and famines. Yet the pestilences can be hidden a little from common view. One of the major pestilences that are now upon us is the disappearance of the honeybee population. Well over half of all honey bees have mysteriously disappeared. This is absolutely critical for the production of our food supplies. The honeybees pollinate plants. Without them there would be a critical shortage of food around the world. I have tried to follow the news on this pestilence. At last word, there was believed to be a nasty bug that was killing off the bees. I had also heard that cell phones were disorienting the bees and they got lost and died. I don't know what the answer is, but it is in the form of a pestilence upon us and it is not the only one.

Beginning Of Sorrows

> **Jesus said: "All these are the beginning of sorrows." Matthew 24:8**

All of the above have taken place and in many instances we can actually see an increase or even an acceleration of these types of events. Yet Jesus taught us that when we see these signs, it is only the *beginning* of the sorrows.

Yet, Jesus' warning of these events is not alone in Scripture. We read the following in the book of 2 Esdras.

> **The angel said to me [the prophet Ezra] "The MOST HIGH has made this world for many, the next world for but a few." 2 Esdras 8:1 (REB)**

> **God told Ezra, "In the last days the inhabitants of the world will be punished for their arrogant lives by prolonged suffering."**
> **2 Esdras 8:50 (REB)**

You will find my discussion and the complete dialogue between God and Ezra in the *Book of Edward, Chapter 21 — [It's a] Myth: Everybody Gets To Go* at http://www.bookofedward.org. You can also find God's discussion with Ezra in 2 Esdras 8:1-9:22. I will not repeat all of it here, but let me just say that everything Jesus has taught us is confirmed by God HIMSELF. And, that it would be well if every living soul understood God's intent about these times.

Ezra asks for understanding of the last days and God provides a similar list to that provided by Jesus above. Listen carefully.

"The angel answered [Ezra]: Keep a careful check; *when you see that some of the signs predicted have already passed, then you will understand that the time has come* for the MOST HIGH to begin to judge the world HE created."
2 Esdras 9:1-2 (REB)

God's Signs of End-Times Beginning

"When the world becomes the scene of earthquakes, insurrections, plots among the nations, unstable government, and panic among rulers, then you will recognize these as the events foretold by the MOST HIGH since first the world began. Just as everything that is done on earth has its beginning and end clearly marked, so it is with the times which the MOST HIGH has determined: the beginning is marked by portents and miracles, the end by manifestations of power." 2 Esdras 9:3-6 (REB)

Signs Table — 2 Esdras 9:3-6

#	REB	NRSV
1	Earthquakes in world	Earthquakes in world
2	Insurrections	Tumult of peoples
3	Plots among nations	Intrigues of nations
4	Unstable government	Wavering of leaders
5	Panic among rulers	Confusion of princes

The five signs of "the beginnings of the End-Times" that God gave the prophet Ezra are fairly similar to the signs Jesus gave us. Jesus specified "famines and pestilences" which do fall into the above categories. And, Jesus gave us an update on deception (intrigues).

Good Deeds & Faith Will Save You

> God told Ezra, "All who come safely through and escape destruction, thanks to their good deeds or the faith they have shown, will survive the dangers I have foretold and witness the salvation I shall bring to my land, the territory I have set apart from all eternity as MY own. Then those who have neglected MY ways will be taken by surprise; their utter contempt for MY ways will bring them lasting torment. All those who in the lifetime failed to acknowledge ME in site of the benefits I brought them, all who disdained MY law while freedom still was theirs, who scornfully dismissed the idea of penitence while the way was still open— all these must learn the truth through torments after death."
>
> **2 Esdras 9:7-12 (REB)**

Going over this dialogue God had with Ezra has me almost in tears again. I can literally hear Ezra pleading with God saying, "The lost outnumber the saved as a wave exceeds a drop of water." It grieves my heart as much as it grieved Ezra's. Yet, I grieve for Christians who have been misled by the Church. When you understand God's criteria and the teachings of Jesus, you will know the Church has led millions astray by failing to accurately teach about repentance and righteousness instead of "mouthing/claiming Jesus as savior."

No amount of mouthing/claiming Jesus as Lord will offset the lack of repentance and righteousness. This is why Jesus rejects "many" Christians in Matthew 7:21-23 and states you will need a minimum amount of righteousness to enter into heaven [God's kingdom].

> **Portent** : ˈpôrˌtent:
> Noun
>
> **1.** A sign or warning that something, esp. something momentous or calamitous, is likely to happen: *they believed that wild birds in the house were portents of death.* • Future significance: *an omen of grave portent for the tribe.* — SOURCE: Apple OSX Dictionary v2.0.2

Beginning Is Marked by <u>Portents and Miracles</u> Or, *Wonders and Mighty Works*

> "The beginnings are manifested in wonders and mighty works, and the end in penalties and in signs." 2 Esdras 9:6 (NRSV)

The *Revised English Version* used the words "portents and miracles," when it talked about the "beginning of the end," but the *New Revised Standard Version* uses the words "wonders and mighty works." Likewise, when describing the end of the End-Times, the contrast is "manifestations of power" and "in penalties and signs." Have you seen any penalties and signs indicating we are coming to the end of the End-Times? You should start looking as I have seen many. I was awestruck by the 9/11 attacks in New York City. I was equally awestruck by hurricanes, which placed a literal X mark across the face of Florida and defied all human logic when doing so from a weather forecasting perspective. Then, there was the direct hit on New Orleans. "In penalties and in signs?"

Aside from what I believe are clear penalties and signs from God, there is the massive deception going on in the USA, which is aided and abetted by a mainstream press as if in a coordinated effort to deceive 300 million people about the nature of what is actually going on. I have never seen such massive and blatant deception, in spite of the ease of communicating truth using the Internet. Yet, along with the ease of distributing truth over the Internet comes a huge amount of deceptive material and propaganda one must first sift through to reach the actual truth from a human perspective. In fact, unless God's Holy Spirit guides you into truth, you will never come to the realization of what is actually going on today. The sheer quantity of information now available is beyond the ability of most people to mentally sort through. Ergo, the mainstream media is highly successful in actually programming people's minds.

So, are we in a societal meltdown in the United States? Or, is this a spiritual meltdown we are experiencing? Is it just bad luck or is God actually moving against man in an End-Times scenario? Were the catastrophic events of 9/11, Florida's X pattern of hurricane destruction and the destruction of New Orleans just bad weather and unfortunate circumstances? Or, were these "penalties and signs" of the Ending of the End-Times taking place? I'll let you make your own decision. I personally believe that we are clearly in the End-Times and that God is trying to get our attention.

To keep us from repentance and returning back to God, Satan has orchestrated a huge media campaign to distract our attention from what is really taking place. Instead of recognizing the spiritual crisis we are now all facing with God in these End-Times, Satan has us mentally focused on economic and other worldly issues.

FATHER, have mercy on all of us and even as Ezra pleaded for souls, I also plead for souls. FATHER, help us all to understand YOUR truth. Open up all of our eyes to YOUR Word.

Ending Is Marked by <u>Manifestations of Power</u> Or, *In Penalties and In Signs*

Study Daniel and the book of Revelation if you want to grasp God's full meaning when HE told Ezra that the ending is marked by "manifestations of power" or " in penalties and in signs."

The scary stuff Jesus said we shouldn't be troubled about, *at the beginning of the End-Times,* will be eclipsed by stuff we'll have a much more difficult time not being scared to death by *during the ending of the End-Times*. Only by knowing whom your God truly is will you be able to endure what is coming to mankind in terms of punishment from God ALMIGHTY.

So, we've seen that the signs of the beginning that both Jesus and God talked about have come true. And, perhaps all the turmoil the United States is going through in its governmental operations is the best telling of some of those signs. Indeed there are many portents of momentous or calamitous things about to happen.

It also seems clear that we have passed by just the "beginning" and are actually into the "penalties and signs" that God told Ezra would accompany the ending of this period of time.

> **"The government of the earth is in the hands of the LORD, he sets the right leader over it at the right time. Human success is in the hands of the LORD." Sirach 10:4-5 (NJB)**

Christians founded our republic on Judeo-Christian values and for ~ 200 years the United States was a Godly nation. Our laws were based on the Bible. As long as we remained faithful to God, we prospered. But now we have become an unfaithful ungodly nation.

Now let's pick up again with Jesus in Matthew 24. We had stopped in verse 8 where Jesus had said, "All these [signs] are the beginning of sorrows." And after this the following will occur.

Then

6. Delivered up to tribulation, killed and hated

"They will deliver you up to tribulation and kill you, and you will be hated by all nations for my name's sake." V9

Are you conscious about all the Christians around the world that are being killed because they believe in Jesus? If not, you should study this, as it is already a reality. And which nation is hated by most other nations? Yes, the Christian nation of the United States. John writes about this teaching of Jesus.

Jesus said: "Yes, the time is coming that whoever kills you will think that he offers God service."
John 16:2

I believe this has occurred over many centuries, but who can miss the current Muslim extremist attempts, in this third millennium, to systematically kill Christians and Jews? Indeed, some Muslims are now waging a holy war against every Christian and Jew. While many Muslims would deny Islam teaches Christians and Jews should be killed, it is the reality on many Muslim streets. In some Muslim countries, Christians are "delivered up to tribulation and even face being killed." In Canada you cannot freely talk about the Bible and homosexuality without running afoul of so-called "hate" laws and getting into tribulation. Ergo, item #6 has come to pass.

And, Then

7. Many will be offended, betraying and hating

"And *then* many will be offended, will betray one another, and will hate one another." V10

In the timing of the End-Time events outlined by Jesus, #6 occurs first and *then* #7 will take place. Therefore, we are now studying a timeline of events disclosed some 2,000 years ago in Scripture, events that are supposed to occur during the End-Times.

After the tribulation and hatred for Christians occurred, especially for Christians in the United States, we find out that offense will occur very easily and that people would betray one another and would hate one another.

This event has also already taken place. There isn't a day that goes by that "offended people" do not become obvious in the news, on television or in families. Betrayal is well documented in the many "tell-all" books that are published seeking monetary gain over any sense of friendship or loyalty to family, friends or one's business. Betrayal is also evidenced in the many television shows where one friend or family member betrays another. Even a vitriol of hatred, spews out in these various television shows and on the news every place one looks. And, if you stand on God's Word as I certainly do, you will offend many people and there is much hatred and betrayal waiting for you. I have experienced all of this. Ergo, it has already taken place and is now taking place all around us.

> "[Know] this first: that scoffers will come in the last days, walking according to their own lusts."
> 2 Peter 3:3

And, Then

8. Many false prophets will deceive many

"*Then* **many** false prophets will ... deceive many." V11

False prophets abound today and it seems like all of them are in "the God business" instead of being "into God's business." They have always been among the people from the time of the original twelve apostles, but now they have multiplied greatly during these End-Times. The operative word in Jesus' teaching above is the word "many." This event has also occurred!

> **"But there were also false prophets among the people, even as there will be false teachers among you, who will secretly bring in destructive heresies, even denying the Lord who bought them, and bring on themselves swift destruction."**
> **2 Peter 2:1**

And, Because

9. Of lawlessness, the love of many will grow cold

"*And because* lawlessness will abound [during this time], the love of many will grow cold." V12

This has also occurred. I have personally experienced it from those whom I love. What does it mean when love grows cold? It means you get the cold shoulder. It means people grow distant from you. It means they might not want to be around you, to talk with you, etc. It is when love turns into indifference and when passion turns into compassion. Indeed, the love of many has grown cold!

But, They Who Endure

10. To the end, shall be saved

"But he who endures to the end shall be saved." V13

Jesus offers us a very big **BUT** after all the troublesome events he has outlined in items 1-9 prior to this point. In a way it represents words of comfort as well as words of guidance. Jesus tells us that if "we can endure" the End-Times, we shall be saved. What does it mean to endure? In means we must remain faithful even unto our own death if needed. If we cannot pass through our own or a loved one's death, remaining in faith, then the faith we have proclaimed is not a real faith in God. Listen to both Jesus and Paul and consider how they reinforce this teaching in Matthew 24:13.

> **Jesus said, "Do not fear any of those things which you are about to suffer. Indeed, the devil is about to throw some of you into prison, that you may be tested, and you will have tribulation ten days. Be faithful until death, and I will give you the crown of life. He, who has an ear, let him hear what the Spirit says to the churches. He who overcomes shall not be hurt by the second death." Revelation 2:10-11**

> **Paul said, "Therefore, my beloved, as you have always obeyed, not as in my presence only, but now much more in my absence, *work out your own salvation with fear and trembling*; for it is God who works in you both to will and to do for His good pleasure." Philippians 2:12**

The End-Times spiritual history we are now going through only promises to get worse. It will get more violent and will literally scare many people to death. This is to say people will experience such tremendous stress and agony during this time, that their bodies will not be able to sustain human life. Yet, we must endure whatever happens in the End-Times if we are to pass into God's kingdom and get saved. Paul's statement: "work out your salvation with fear and trembling" is what every Christian needs to be aware of and they must know NOW. This critical guidance from Jesus and Paul is not something taught in the typical church. You *will* have to endure everything that is coming and only God knows what that is.

Gospel Of The Kingdom
Will be preached in the entire world!

So everything I have talked about so far, from the teachings of Jesus, has already come to pass. This brings us up to the point of the NEXT CRITICAL EVENT in God's spiritual timeline. It is the preaching of the gospel of the kingdom. Listen carefully.

> **Jesus said, "And this gospel of the kingdom will be preached in all the world as a witness to all the nations and then the end will come."**
> **Matthew 24:14**

So, if you are a Christian, let me ask you this question. Have you heard a message concerning the "gospel of the kingdom?" Or, have you just heard about Jesus Christ? Have you heard how God came down and took the form of a man and died on the cross? I believe you've heard a lot about Jesus and about the myth of God on the cross, but that you know little about the "gospel of the kingdom."

Am I right? Have you ever heard about Jesus' gospel? Well, this is the event in which we are now in and are awaiting completion. It is literally where we are at in God's spiritual timeline of the End-Times. Everything Jesus has taught so far has come true, but not this particular event. Jesus has been preached in the entire world, but his message of "the gospel of the kingdom" has not been preached in the entire world. Not even in all of the United States.

This Gospel Preaching Is Now Unfolding!
You still have time to get right with God.

The word "gospel" is widely understood to mean "good news." The typical evangelist would ask, "Have you heard the good news?" He or she would then probably educate the person on the sacrificial death of Jesus Christ, God's only human begotten Son. He or she may then continue on into mythology by stating something like, "God knew you couldn't do it all by yourself, so HE came down and died on the cross for you."

The first part is true. Jesus died a sacrificial death on the cross just like any other human being would have suffered if they had been on the cross. Jesus' death was predestined as a final sacrifice for the sins of the world. The second part about "God on the cross" is mythology created by the Church. Yet, in all of this, where is any part of the gospel Jesus wanted "preached in all the world?"

To paraphrase Jesus, "The good news about the kingdom of God will be preached in all the world as a witness to all the nations and then the end will come." As the Spirit is with me, God has told me that this does not mean that all the people in all the nations of the world will be preached this gospel. Instead, this gospel will be preached throughout the world only as a witness to the "nations."

We don't have to wonder about what the gospel of Jesus is all about or what his purpose on earth was really about. Jesus fully explained his purpose on this earth and what he preached about.

> **Jesus said: "I must preach the kingdom of God to the other cities also, because for this purpose I have been sent [to earth]." Luke 4:43**

We see Christ confirming that the "gospel of the kingdom" really refers to the "kingdom of God." We also see that preaching this message is why Jesus was sent to earth. We then read in Matthew 4 what the essence of Christ's message was.

> **"From that time Jesus began to preach and to say, 'Repent, for the kingdom of heaven is at hand.' " Matthew 4:17**

Many Christians believe that if they can say with their mouth "Jesus is my Lord" that they are saved. Yet, Jesus did not preach that message nor is it to be found anywhere in the New Testament. The message Jesus taught was the same as the message John the Baptist taught. It was a message of repentance. It was the same message of all of God's prophets from time immemorial. Virtually nothing has changed from God's message.

To repent means to turn away from wickedness and the ways of this world and turn back to God and to HIS ways. The gospel of repentance *for God's kingdom is near* has not been preached yet. Furthermore, the Church has corrupted the message of God through the mouth of Jesus. Ergo, the message of Jesus has not been taught even though Jesus has been taught. Time is closing fast and "the kingdom is near." It is a good day, today, to repent unto God and to ask for HIS strength during these End-Times. We will need HIM to get through it all.

Then, The End Will Come

So after you see the spiritual message of the Church shifting from Jesus' death on the cross to a demand for repentance, righteousness and a return to God's ways *preached* in the world as a witness to the nations -- then the end *will* come. When the completion of the preaching of the gospel message of Christ occurs I do not know. However, the completion of this *preaching* event unleashes the final ending events in the End-Times spiritual timeline.

> **"Therefore, when you see the *'abomination of desolation'* spoken of by Daniel the prophet, standing in the holy place (whoever reads, let him understand), then let those who are in Judea flee to the mountains." Matthew 24:15**

The *abomination of desolation* is the antichrist sitting in the holy temple of God and pretending he is God. Christ instructs us:

Warnings

1. If you are in Judea, flee to the mountains. V16
2. If you are on the housetop, don't come down. V17
3. Don't try to take anything out of the house. V17
4. If you are in the field, don't go get any clothes. V18
5. Woe to those pregnant or nursing babies. V19
6. Pray your flight is not in winter or on the Sabbath. V20
7. There will be great tribulation, never seen before. V21
8. The great tribulation will not be seen again. V21
9. Unless these days were shortened, no human lives. V22
10. For the elect's sake, the days will be shortened. V22
11. Don't believe claims that Christ is here or there. V23
12. False Christs and prophets will show great signs. V24
13. Attempts to deceive even the elect take place. V24
14. See, you have been told ahead of time. V25
15. Don't believe them if they say Jesus is here or there. V26

After, The Tribulation

More terrifying events occur immediately after the tribulation. In this case, it sounds almost like a nuclear winter or the aftermath of massive nuclear war. Will humans even exist without the Sun? Listen to the terrifying description that Jesus provides.

> "Immediately *after* the tribulation of those days the sun will be darkened, and the moon will not give its light; the stars will fall from Heaven, and the powers of the heavens will be shaken."
> Matthew 24:29

Then, Son of Man Sign

Jesus warns us not to be deceived by thinking he is in the desert or in one of the inner rooms or for that matter anywhere else. Why? It is because he tells us that we will see the event in the sky. That he will literally be descending from heaven on the clouds.

> "For as the lightning comes from the east and flashes to the west, so also will the coming of the Son of Man be." Matthew 24:27

> "Then the sign of the Son of Man will appear in heaven, and then all the tribes of the earth will mourn, and they will see the Son of Man coming on the clouds of Heaven with power and great glory." Matthew 24:30

Jesus teaches us that all the tribes of the earth "will see the Son of Man coming on the clouds of heaven." How will that happen? The Hubble space telescope combined with the Internet and Cable news? Clearly, the technology exists to broadcast such an event.

Parable of Fig Tree

Jesus teaches we will know the season of these events in his parable of the fig tree. See Matthew 24:32-34

> **"When you see all these things [events], know that it is near, at the very doors." Matthew 24:33**

Analogy of Noah's Days

Jesus teaches most people will be surprised and caught off guard by his second coming. He also issues several warnings to us. See Matthew 24:36-44.

> **"But as the days of Noah were, so also will the coming of the Son of Man be." Matthew 24:37**

More Warnings

1. It will surprise and shock mankind. V36
2. Only the FATHER knows when the event will occur. V36
3. People will be playing and just ignoring God. V37
4. Most will be mortally too late, just like in the flood. V39
5. 50% of those in the field will disappear. V40
6. 50% of those in the field will be left on the earth. V40
7. 50% of those in the mill will disappear. V41
8. Those who disappear will be "raptured" by God.
9. Being raptured means taken out of harm's way.
10. 50% of those in the mill will be left on the earth. V41
11. Watch carefully, because you don't know the time. V42
12. Be on your guard, mindful that it could be anytime. V43
13. Be ready for the Son of Man comes unexpectedly. V44

Analogy of the Two Servants

Jesus teaches that if we are truly faithful, we will be found doing righteous things when he returns. Those whom Jesus finds faithful will be blessed upon his return. Those whom Jesus finds unfaithful upon his return will suffer greatly. See Matthew 24:45-50

> **"The master of [the unfaithful] servant will come on a day when he is not looking for him and at an hour he is not aware of. [Because the servant is caught being unfaithful, the master] will cut him in two and appoint him his portion with the hypocrites. There shall be weeping and gnashing of teeth." Matthew 24:50**

Summary of Matthew 24

Matthew 24 represents a spiritual timeline of End-Times events that have already occurred or are *now* unfolding upon mankind. We are presently awaiting the completion of the "preaching of the gospel of the kingdom to the world." Once that is completed, the end of this spiritual age comes. Terrifying events will ensue.

We will have to be strong spiritually and in faith to survive the End-Times events. It will become so bad, that God's punishment will have to be cut short so that "the elect of God may survive."

Maybe you have been led to believe that there is nothing to do but claim Jesus as your Lord and savior, but the Church has misled you. Consider Jesus' teachings in Matthew 24 seriously and tell all of your family to be prepared. To fully see what is happening, you will have to shift your focus from worldly to spiritual events.

Matthew 25

[1] "Then the kingdom of heaven shall be likened to ten virgins who took their lamps and went out to meet the bridegroom. [2] Now five of them were wise, and five were foolish. [3] Those who were foolish took their lamps and took no oil with them, [4] but the wise took oil in their vessels with their lamps. [5] But while the bridegroom was delayed, they all slumbered and slept. [6] And at midnight a cry was heard: 'Behold, the bridegroom is coming; go out to meet him!' [7] Then all those virgins arose and trimmed their lamps. [8] And the foolish said to the wise, 'Give us some of your oil, for our lamps are going out.' [9] But the wise answered, saying, 'No, lest there should not be enough for us and you; but go rather to those who sell, and buy for yourselves.' [10] And while they went to buy, the bridegroom came, and those who were ready went in with him to the wedding; and the door was shut. [11] Afterward, the other virgins came also, saying, 'Lord, Lord, open to us!' [12] But he answered and said, 'Assuredly, I say to you, I do not know you.' [13] Watch therefore, for you know neither the day nor the hour in which the Son of Man is coming."

[14] "For the kingdom of heaven is like a man traveling to a far country, who called his own servants and delivered his goods to them. [15] And to one he gave five talents, to another two, and to another one, to each according to his own ability; and immediately he went on a journey. [16] Then he who had received the five talents went and traded with them, and made another five talents. [17] And likewise he who had received two gained two more also. [18] But he who had received one went and dug in the ground, and hid his lord's money. [19] After a long time the lord of those servants came and settled accounts with them. [20] So he who had received five talents came and brought five other talents, saying, 'Lord, you delivered to me five talents; look, I have gained five more talents besides them.' "

[21] "His lord said to him, 'Well done, good and faithful servant; you were faithful over a few things, I will make you ruler over many things. Enter into the joy of your lord.' [22] He also who had received two talents came and said, 'Lord, you delivered to me two talents; look, I have gained two more talents besides them.' [23] His lord said to him, 'Well done, good and faithful servant; you have been faithful over a few things, I will make you ruler over many things. Enter into the joy of your lord.' "

[24] "Then he who had received the one talent came and said, 'Lord, I knew you to be a hard man, reaping where you have not sown, and gathering where you have not scattered seed. [25] And I was afraid, and went and hid your talent in the ground. Look, there you have what is yours.' [26] But his lord answered and said to him, 'You wicked and lazy servant, you knew that I reap where I have not sown, and gather where I have not scattered seed. [27] So you ought to have deposited my money with the bankers, and at my coming I would have received back my own with interest."

[28] "Therefore take the talent from him, and give it to him who has ten talents. [29] For to everyone who has, more will be given, and he will have abundance; but from him who does not have, even what he has will be taken away. [30] And cast the unprofitable servant into the outer darkness. There will be weeping and gnashing of teeth.' "

[31] "When the Son of Man comes in His glory, and all the holy angels with him, then he will sit on the throne of his glory. [32] All the nations will be gathered before him [Christ], and he [Christ] will separate them one from another, as a shepherd divides his sheep from the goats. [33] And he will set the sheep on his right hand, but the goats on the left."

[34] "Then the King [Christ] will say to those on his right hand, 'Come, you blessed of my FATHER, inherit the kingdom prepared for you from the foundation of the world: [35] for I was hungry and you gave me food; I was thirsty and you gave me drink; I was a stranger and you took me in; [36] I was naked and you clothed me; I was sick and you visited me; I was in prison and you came to me.' [37] Then the righteous will answer him, saying, 'Lord, [Jesus] when did we see you hungry and feed you, or thirsty and give you drink? [38] When did we see you a stranger and take you in, or naked and clothe you? [39] Or when did we see you sick, or in prison, and come to you?' [40] And the King [Christ] will answer and say to them, 'Assuredly, I say to you, inasmuch as you did it to one of the least of these my brethren, you did it to me.'"

[41] "Then he [Christ] will also say to those on the left hand, 'Depart from me, you cursed, into the everlasting fire prepared for the devil and his angels: [42] for I was hungry and you gave me no food; I was thirsty and you gave me no drink; [43] I was a stranger and you did not take me in, naked and you did not clothe me, sick and in prison and you did not visit me.' [44] Then they also will answer him, saying, 'Lord, [Jesus] when did we see you hungry or thirsty or a stranger or naked or sick or in prison, and did not minister to you?' [45] Then he [Christ] will answer them, saying, 'Assuredly, I say to you, inasmuch as you did not do it to one of the least of these, you did not do it to me.' [46] And these will go away into everlasting punishment, but the righteous into eternal life."

Jesus' End-Times Teachings In Matthew 25

Jesus continues with his End-Times' instructions in Matthew 25. This time, however, it is not about listing events and providing us with a timeline. Instead, Jesus teaches us about the importance of our personal behavior.

If our faith is sincere towards God, our behavior demonstrates this spiritual reality. Our behavior needs to be godly and righteous in the eyes of our God. Jesus teaches us to, "be ready for the events that are unexpected." Jesus teaches us to, "be faithful servants" of all that God has given us. And, he teaches us, "to be caring" of those who are less fortunate than we are. This would mean helping to take care of those within our sphere of influence in terms of family, friends and community. Pitching in where we know we can help make a difference.

In all of his teachings, Jesus is giving us a heads up that our deeds will count. Therefore, our faith, righteousness and behavior matters to God and we cannot just call on Jesus as our Lord and savior expecting it alone saves us. James confirms this spiritual reality.

> **"But do you want to know, O foolish man, that faith without works is dead?" James 2:20**

> **"For as the body without the spirit is dead, so faith without works is dead also." James 2:26**

This section in Matthew also gives more weight to Jesus' statement about being faithful *even* unto our own death. It means we do not accept the idea of "cheap grace" or salvation without a price. This is discussed further in the chapter titled, *The Unfaithful*.

The Ten Virgins

This parable continues an amazing 50% factor when it comes to salvation. Literally 50% of the ten virgins did not get to go with the bridegroom. Ergo, they did not make it into heaven. It is similar to the 50% Jesus tells us in Matthew 24 that are left in the fields and the 50% that are left in the mills. The other 50% of people made it into heaven because they were ready; they were prepared. A more detailed discussion of Jesus' 50% factor can be found in Chapter 21 of the *Book of Edward* at http://www.bookofedward.org.

The message here is simple. Be prepared, as Jesus will return at an unexpected time. Literally 50% or half of all people who say they believe in Jesus will not be ready when Jesus returns. That is the teaching of Jesus. Yet, I personally believe the percentage will be a lot higher. In this parable, Jesus says, "The kingdom of heaven will be *likened* to ten virgins." So, even though he states a 50% factor, that does not mean it is exactly 50%. It only means it is large!

Half of the virgins failed to bring extra oil for their lamps and were running out when the bridegroom showed up. Instead of going to the bridegroom, they first had to go get oil. When they returned, they were locked out. In this analogy, Jesus literally means they were locked out of heaven because they were not ready to go.

> **[After getting the oil to keep their lamps going, the] "Other virgins came also, saying, 'Lord, Lord, open to us!' But he answered and said, 'Assuredly, I say to you, I do not know you.'"**
> **Matthew 5:11-12**

Jesus said, "I never knew you" in Matthew 7:21-23 when he rejects lawless Christians who called him "Lord, Lord." Similar thing, isn't it? If we know him, we obey him. When we do that, we are ready.

The Profitable Servants

In Matthew 25:14-30 we find the parable of the talents. In this story, the master of three servants gives one 5 talents [money], another 2 talents and a third 1 talent. It was their responsibility to the master to take care of his property and to properly manage it.

When the master comes home, the first two servants were profitable for him actually doubling the talents to 10 and 4 respectively. The third servant simply buried the 1 talent he received and then returned it to the master without gain. This third servant was unprofitable to his master. He failed to take care of what was given to him in this life. As a result he was punished.

> **"And cast the unprofitable servant into the outer darkness. There will be weeping and gnashing of teeth." Matthew 25:30**

The unprofitable servant gets punished and "cast into the outer darkness," but the master blesses the profitable servants. They are even made RULERS over many things because they were faithful over a few things.

> **"His lord said [to the profitable servants] 'Well done, good and faithful servant; you have been faithful over a few things, I will make you ruler over many things. Enter into the joy of your lord.' " Matthew 25:21, 23.**

Jesus teaches us that we must be faithful even in the smallest of things of this life. If we are faithful in the small things, we will be given much more. However, if we are found unfaithful in small things and especially in anything involving money, we will be cast aside as unfaithful.

The End-Times Selection Process

Jesus explains the process in which people will be selected and judged, at the "End of Days," in Matthew 25:31-46. Jesus separates out the righteous people from the wicked people *and from all nations* at the end. Therefore, a selection and sorting process takes place at the very end just prior to Christ's final judgment.

> **"All the nations will be gathered before [Jesus], and he will separate them one from another, as a shepherd divides his sheep from the goats. And he will set the sheep [righteous people] on his right, but the goats [unrighteous people] on the left."**
>
> **"Then the King [Jesus] will say to those on his right hand, 'Come, you blessed of my FATHER [our God], inherit the kingdom prepared for you from the foundation of the world." Matthew 25:32-34**

I have heard it preached that this "sorting" of the nations is only going to apply to those who claim Jesus as Lord. In this thought, everyone except those exposed to Jesus are lost souls. However, this is not true and such teaching reflects Christian mythology that the only way to heaven is through Jesus Christ. This teaches against Scripture and presumes there is no righteousness outside of Christ. Yet, a lot of Scripture, and especially this one, teaches that salvation belongs to the righteous. Not to those who mouth Jesus.

> **"Then Peter opened his mouth and said: In truth I perceive that God shows no partiality. But in every nation whoever fears HIM and works righteousness is accepted by HIM." Acts 10:34**

Therefore, salvation is more tied to repentance and righteousness than to any verbal statement such as "Jesus is my Lord and savior."

The End-Times Judgment

After Jesus says, "Come you blessed of my FATHER," he gives us six additional criteria that were used in his selection process.

Jesus tells the righteous in Matthew 25:35-36

1. You fed me when I was hungry
2. You gave me drink when I was thirsty
3. You took me in when I was a stranger
4. You clothed me when I was naked
5. You visited me when I was sick
6. You visited me when I was in prison

The righteous ask Jesus

> **"Then the righteous will answer [Jesus], saying, 'Lord, when did we see you hungry and feed you, or thirsty and give your drink? When did we see you a stranger and take you in, or naked and clothe you? Or when did we see you sick, or in prison, and come to you?" Matthew 25:37-39**

Jesus explains to them

> **"And the King will answer and say to them, 'Assuredly, I say to you, inasmuch as you did it to one of the least of these my brethren, you did it to me." Matthew 25:40**

What does this tell us? It clearly tells us that righteous people look outward during this life and not inward. It means they take time to care about others and would generally be considered unselfish. The above list of six fundamental human needs applies to *every* human. There isn't a single one of us that hasn't witnessed these needs or sufferings among those we could help in our sphere of influence.

Unrighteous People Condemned

Jesus tells the unrighteous in Matthew 25:41-43, **"Depart from me you cursed, into the everlasting fire prepared for the devil and his angels."** He then says to the unrighteous...

You did not:

1. Feed me when I was hungry
2. Give me drink when I was thirsty
3. Take me in when I was a stranger
4. Clothe me when I was naked
5. Visit me when I was sick
6. Visit me when I was in prison

The unrighteous ask Jesus

> **"Then [the unrighteous] will also answer him saying, 'Lord, when did we see you hungry or thirsty or a stranger or naked or sick or in prison, and did not minister to you?"**
> **Matthew 25:44**

Jesus explains to them

> **"And [Jesus] will answer them, saying, 'Assuredly, I say to you, inasmuch as you did not do it to one of the least of these, you did not do it to me." Matthew 25:45**

> **"And these [the unrighteous] will go away into everlasting punishment, but the righteous into eternal life." Matthew 25:46**

Choose carefully whom you will believe.
Choose To Believe Jesus!

Summary of Matthew 25

Matthew 25 represents a continuation of the End-Times teachings of Jesus. However, in contrast to the prior chapter, which specified events and presented a spiritual timeline to us—Matthew 25 talks directly to us about specific types of behavior. Our behavior and deeds must be righteous in God's eyes. Jesus helps us understand what it means to be righteous in God's eyes. We are taught that the following are key behavioral traits of righteous people:

1. They are spiritually prepared with readiness behavior.
2. They are profitable and fruitful servants of God.
3. They have an outward look upon life that allows them to assist others in need within their sphere of influence.

In all of the criteria focused on our behavior, as discussed by Jesus, did you see even one mention of being able to "mouth Jesus" or to claim him as our Lord and savior? Why not? The answer is simple. Jesus never taught us that this was any of God's criteria. You won't find a single Scripture in the bible that relates your ability to say Jesus is Lord to salvation. It doesn't exist. This will become clearer as you read the rest of this book.

What you will find is that Jesus was sent to help us get home and that a sincere belief in Jesus results in a return to God along with the righteous behavior that will get us saved and into "eternal life." The apostle Paul confirms this in Romans 10:10 when he teaches, "For with the heart one believes to righteousness." Ergo, if there is no righteousness, there is no salvation.

I have included two graphics below which summarize the selection process and who comes into judgment. Not everyone is judged!

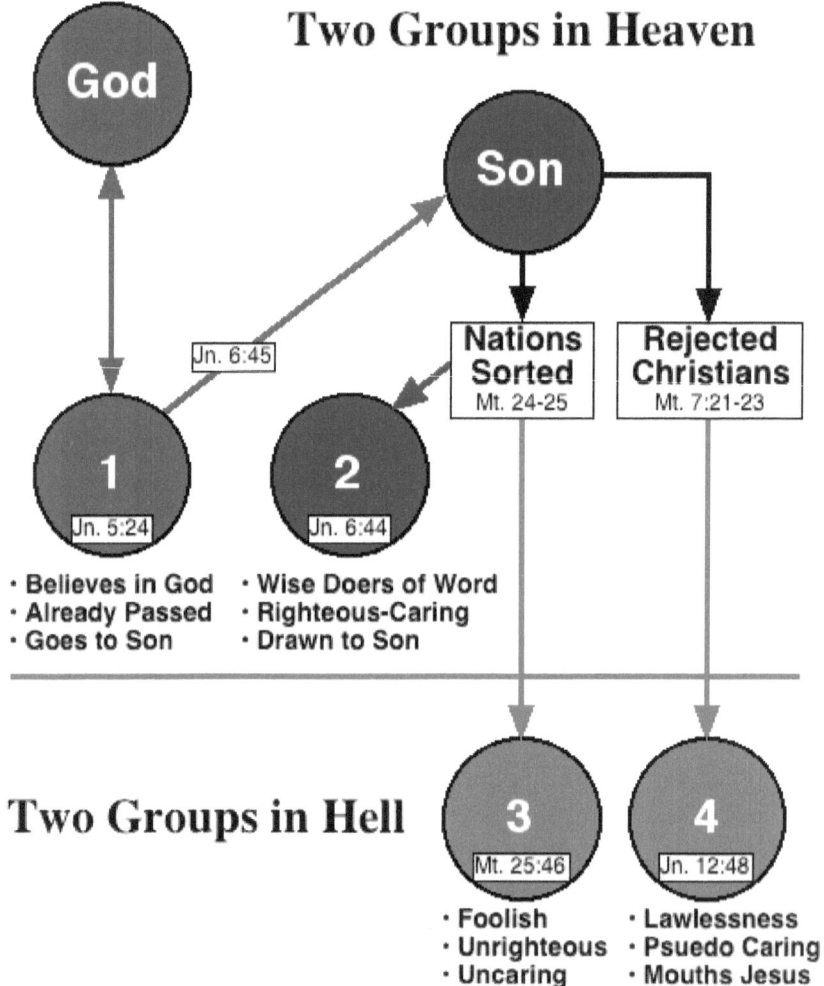

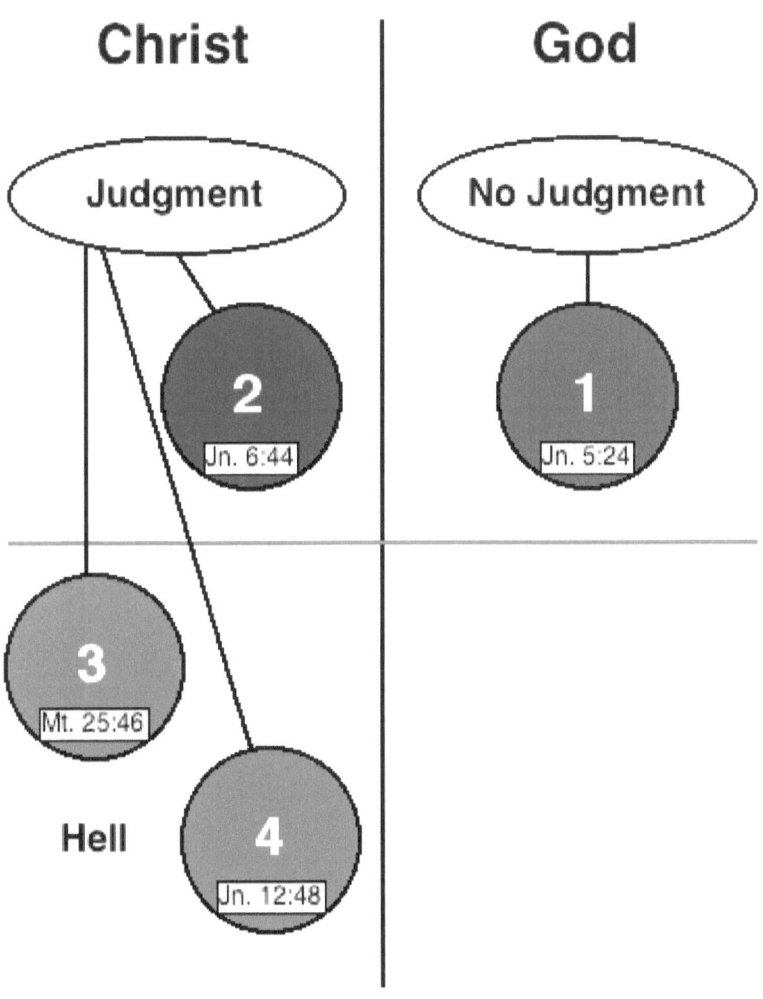

The Invitation

> **Behold, Jesus stands at the door of your heart and knocks. If you hear his voice and will open up your heart, his spirit and God's Spirit will come in and dwell with your spirit and you will become one with them. They will help you overcome this earthly life, so that you can be with them in heaven for an eternal life when your earthly journey ends.**
>
> **Apostle Edward**

Bible Verses: Revelation 3:20-21; John 14:23; 1 John 4:9

The Invitation Contents

	Page
The Invitation	39
Open Up Your Heart	41
All Of Your Heart	41
Exercise Your Faith	42
Become Born Again	42
Jesus' Instructions To Paul	43
Four Expectations of Christ	43-44
Obedience Expectation of God	44
Knowing The God Christ Served	45
Get God's Identify Right	46
Paul Identifies God As The FATHER	47
Becoming One In Spirit	48
Give God A Loyal Heart	48-49
We are Born Again Through The Word of God	49
Paul's Born Again Formula	50
Don't Miss Part II	50-51
Minimum Righteousness Standard	51
Falling In Love With God	52-55
Prayer To Accept God's Invitation	56
The Apostle Edward	57
Two Heart Gateways	58

Open Up Your Heart

Exactly what does it mean to open up your heart to God and HIS only begotten human Son Jesus? Well, it's really quite simple if you think about it. Doesn't everyone you love occupy a special place "in your heart" where joy, happiness, sadness and even heartache or heartbreak can occur?

When you choose to love someone, you open up your heart to all the emotions associated with that love. The same thing occurs with God. HE wants to be in that special place called your heart. Jesus gives us a second chance offer by knocking on the door of our hearts asking us to "open up."

Hello! Do you know that life begins after our earthly journey ends? Do you know about "The Invitation" from God?

All Of Your Heart

God sent Jesus to remind us once again that the "kingdom of heaven" is real. That there is an afterlife for those who will repent and return back to God. Jesus was not the first to offer us this invitation to an eternal life.

> **God said: "You will find ME when you search for ME with all your heart!" Jeremiah 29:13**

In order for you to search for God with all your heart, you'll have to acknowledge that God exists and step into the realm of faith.

> **"But without faith it is impossible to please HIM, for he who comes to God must believe that HE is [exists], and that HE is a rewarder of those who diligently seek HIM." Hebrews 11:6**

Exercise Your Faith

You approach God with your whole heart in faith. Exercising faith means you do not have all the answers. If you had the answers, you would not need to exercise faith/hope.

> **"Now faith is the substance of things hoped for, the evidence of things not seen." Hebrews 11:1**

> **"Faith comes by hearing, and hearing by the word of God." Romans 10:17**

The more you know God's Word, the easier it is to exercise faith. Only by exercising faith can you become born-again. You were first **born of a woman** [flesh]. Becoming born again means that you are **born of the Spirit** by returning to and acknowledging your God, our Creator.

You return to God by exercising the faith of a child, by accepting God's Word as truth.

Become Born Again

Many preach that you are born again by accepting Jesus Christ as your Savior. However, this is not the complete truth of salvation. Accepting Christ as savior must go beyond just mouthing him as Lord.

> **Jesus said: "Not everyone who says to me, 'Lord, Lord' shall enter the kingdom of heaven, but he who does the will of my FATHER [God] in heaven." Matthew 7:21**

Jesus rejects many Christians who claim that he is their savior. We don't have to guess why, because Jesus tells us why in verse 23.

> **Jesus said: "I will declare to them [those people who Christ rejects], I never knew you; depart from me, you who practice lawlessness."**
> **Matthew 7:23**

Jesus' Instructions To Paul

So, in Jesus' own words, we see that just claiming him, as savior with our mouths, is not enough in spite of what many people preach. Paul explains to King Agrippa in Acts the instructions he received from Jesus.

> **Jesus said: "I now send you [to the Gentiles] to open their eyes and to turn them from darkness to light; and from the power of Satan to God, that they may receive forgiveness of sins and an inheritance among those who are sanctified by faith in me." Acts 26:17-18**

So, in Christ's mind, you have at least FOUR things to do to get your inheritance, which is an eternal life in heaven. This is the invitation I am talking about.

Four Expectations Of Christ

1. **You open up your eyes.** This means you open up your heart and listen to God and HIS Son Jesus. That you take to your heart the message now being given.

2. **You turn from darkness to light.** This means that you focus on God's ways, not on man's ways.

3. **You turn from the power of Satan to God.** This means that you repent of your sins and tap into the power of God. It means that you choose to become one with God and HIS Son Jesus.

4. **You are sanctified by faith in Jesus.** This means you are made holy before God's eyes because you have chosen to believe in God's only begotten human Son – Jesus Christ of Nazareth. Your faith is then followed by obedience.

Obedience Expectation Of God

"For God so loved the world that HE gave HIS only begotten [human] Son, that whosoever believes in him [Jesus] should not perish, but have everlasting life." John 3:16

What a wonderful verse this is, but if you stopped here in John, you would miss the message in verse 36.

"He who believes in the Son [Jesus] has everlasting life, and he who does not believe the Son shall not see life, but the wrath of God abides on him." John 3:36

Some bibles state the last part clearer in that the wrath of God abides on those who do not obey the Son. Therefore, you must not only believe in Jesus, but you must believe what he taught and obey his commands.

Knowing The God Christ Served

Many Christians have been misled by false doctrines and no longer know the God that Christ served. Worse, they have mistakenly substituted Christ as their God. We know this because the manmade tradition called the "trinity doctrine" has negated the actual teachings of Jesus Christ and Paul in many churches. Listen carefully, it's important.

> **Jesus said: "He who believes in me, believes not in me, but in HIM who sent me." John 12:44**

If you are a true believer in Jesus, you listen to his words and you have returned back to his FATHER, our God. That means you know the FATHER, God Almighty, who is known as YAHWEH, JEHOVAH, LORD, and also designated in Hebrew texts by the four characters YWHW. LORD replaces YWHW in bibles to designate God.

> **Jesus said: "I am ascending to my FATHER and your FATHER, and to my God and your God."**
> **John 20:17**

These are very simple words from Jesus. He speaks of the God we all serve, including he himself. However, many who believe in the trinity doctrine, cannot accept these words as they are written. Perverse doctrines now distort and twist the words of Christ for the purpose of leading people to hell. Is it important to know the God that Christ served? Yes, it is, and the Apostle Paul tells us why in 2 Thessalonians 1:8.

> **"When the Lord Jesus is revealed from heaven with God's mighty angels, in flaming fire [Christ will] take vengeance on A) those who do not know God, and on B) those who do not obey the gospel of our Lord Jesus Christ." 2 Thessalonians 1:8**

Get God's Identity Right

Seven Bible Teachings:

1. Christ is our High Priest. Hebrews 7:16-17

2. In all things, Christ had to be made like his human brethren so that he could be an effective High Priest. Hebrews 2:17

3. Those who do not believe Christ and obey Christ are not really saved. John 3:36

4. Christ taught us to worship and serve only the FATHER, "his God and our God." Matthew 4:10

5. Christ taught us to pray only to the FATHER, "his God and our God." John 4:23-24; Matthew 6:6

6. Christ taught us that he was the first of God's creations. Revelation 3:14

7. There are seven Spirits of God. Revelation 1:4

"**Fear God** [who Jesus and Paul identified as the FATHER] and give glory to HIM, for the hour of HIS judgment has come; and worship HIM who made heaven and earth, the sea and springs of water." Revelation 14:7

Paul Identifies God As *The* FATHER

Jesus taught us that the FATHER was his God and also our God. The Apostle Paul taught us the same thing about God in 1 Corinthians chapter 8!

ONE GOD, THE FATHER

> "There is no other God but one. For even if there are so-called gods, whether in heaven or on earth (as there are many gods and many lords), yet for us ...
>
> There is only one God, the FATHER of whom are all things and we for HIM; and

ONE LORD, JESUS CHRIST

> One Lord Jesus Christ, through whom are all things, and through whom we live."
>
> 1 Corinthians 8:4-6

This means we are of God and created by HIM, but we live through Christ Jesus and by faith in Christ we are obedient to God.

It is our faith in Christ that welcomes his spirit and the Spirit of his God into our heart. When we operate in faith, without having all the human answers, the door to our heart opens wide to our savior Jesus and his God. It is our obedience to God that then allows us to overcome this world.

Becoming One In Spirit

The spirits of my wife Jackie and I became one-flesh. Of course, we were not literally one flesh, but in spiritual terms we were one flesh. We were of the same mind, the same spirit and because of this we thought alike on almost everything. We were not robots. Both of us had different opinions at times, but still, we were basically of one mind.

Because we were one with each other, we often completed each other's sentences and even knew what the other was thinking long before any words were spoken. I often could hear her voice speaking to me or hear her mind thinking about me. The same thing occurred with her.

I cannot fully explain this in human terms, because it is a spiritual mystery that comes into play when a love bond is very strong between two people. However, many who made a commitment to love for a lifetime can testify to the wonderment that they were of one-flesh with their spouse.

After my wife Jackie died in 2003, I could still hear her thoughts. I knew what she would think in every situation. For example: When I reached for the wrong shirt, I could even hear her in my mind saying: "You can't wear that shirt with those pants."

Give God A Loyal Heart

Jackie and I got to this place of wonderment of being one-flesh by giving all of our heart to each other. Our hearts were committed and unquestionably loyal to each other. God wants nothing less than a committed and loyal heart from you. If your heart is loyal and committed to HIM, you will be amazed at the adventure HE will bring to your life.

The Eyes of God Searches For Loyal Hearts

"For the eyes of the LORD [God] run to and fro throughout the whole earth, to show HIMSELF strong on behalf of those whose heart is loyal [committed] to HIM." 2 Chronicles 16:9

Think about this! God Almighty will show HIMSELF strong on your behalf if you give HIM a loyal heart. It all starts when you just open up your heart in faith to HIS Son Jesus.

We Are Born Again
Through The Word of God

You'll find the phrase born again used in the Bible in three locations: John 3:3, 3:7; and, in 1 Peter 1:23. Jesus talking to Nicodemus confirms in John 3:3 that you will need to be born again to enter the kingdom of God. In John 3:7-8, Jesus confirms that being born again means that you are born of the Spirit.

Peter teaches us that becoming "born again" comes through the "incorruptible word of God."

> "Since you have purified your souls in obeying the truth through the Spirit in sincere love of the brethren, love one another fervently with a pure heart, having been born again, not of corruptible seed but incorruptible, through the word of God, which lives and abides forever." 1 Peter 1:22-23

Paul's Born Again Formula

"But what does it say? 'The word is near you, even in your mouth and in your heart.' (That is, the word of faith which we preach): that if you confess with your mouth the Lord Jesus and believe in your heart that God has raised him from the dead, you will be saved. For with the heart one believes to righteousness and with the mouth confession is made to salvation."
Romans 10:8-10

*Two parts to Paul's born again formula.

I) You confess with your mouth that God raised Jesus from the dead [you believe in the resurrection]; and,

II) You believe in your heart unto God's righteousness. You want to do what is right in God's eyes.

Don't Miss Part II

Many ministries promote a message that all you have to do is "mouth" that Jesus is your Lord and savior and you then have eternal life. You can now see that Jesus preached a different message and that Paul's salvation formula is two parts and not just one part where you "mouth Jesus as your Lord."

Many people ignore part II of Paul's teaching!

Anyone who fully accepts Christ returns back to God, our FATHER, and truly knows God and the fact that Jesus is not God. They do not worship Jesus or even pray to Jesus. They obey what Jesus taught them: Worship only the FATHER, our God; and, Pray to only the FATHER in Jesus' name. We pray to God in Jesus' name to honor his sacrifice on the cross and because he is our Teacher.

Part II is belief in our hearts unto God's righteousness. In other words, we become obedient to God's righteousness standard.

Jesus Teaches There Is A Minimum Righteousness Standard We Must Exceed Before Entering Heaven

Jesus said: "For I say to you, that unless your righteousness exceeds the righteousness of the scribes and Pharisees, you will by no means enter the kingdom of heaven." Matthew 5:20

In the above verse, Jesus clearly teaches us there is a minimum righteousness standard to get into heaven. Our righteousness must exceed that of the scribes and Pharisees. They often pretended to be righteous with God, but instead were wicked; they were hypocrites.

Righteousness simply means you do what is right in God's eyes. Often this can be contrasted as being opposite of what is right in man's eyes. We know what God expects from us because the Bible tells us all about God's character and HIS likes and dislikes.

Falling In Love With God

Many believe the Bible is all about Jesus, but this is not true. These people fail to acknowledge Jesus was another messenger from God. The real story in the Bible is a great love story about our God who created us and loved us so much that HE would send and sacrifice HIS only human Son in a final attempt to give us "The Invitation."

> **Jesus said: "I must preach the kingdom of God to the other cities also, because for this purpose I have been sent." Luke 4:43**
>
> **"For many deceivers have gone out into the world who do not confess Jesus Christ as coming in the flesh. This is a deceiver and an antichrist." 2 John 7**

To become saved, your mouth must confess the humanity [coming in the flesh], the death on the cross and the resurrection of Jesus.

> **"And we know that the Son of God [Jesus Christ] has come and has given us an understanding that we may know HIM [God, the FATHER] who is true; and we are in HIM [God, the FATHER] who is true, [if we are] in HIS Son Jesus Christ. This [GOD, the FATHER] is the true God and eternal life." 1 John 5:20**

If you accept Jesus Christ in your heart as savior, he has brought you back to his God. You have, like I did – fallen in love with our Creator God who seeks fellowship with us. At this point, you'll be excited about your future eternity and you'll want to know more. You'll be hungry for God's Word and will read the entire Bible.

It was over 31-years ago that I fell in love with God. Struggling with life seemed like the never ending story of my existence until one day God touched my life in a way that I absolutely knew H<small>E</small> was real.

The Invitation asks you to acknowledge that there is more going on in this earthly life than what your human senses can detect. There is another side to this life, a spiritual side. Unless you become born again in the spirit, you cannot begin to understand or for that matter even perceive the full truth that exists in this earthly life.

Events in life happen for many reasons, but often those reasons have a spiritual basis. God sent H<small>IS</small> Son as a final sacrifice for the sins of mankind. In the process, God left us with an opportunity to step out in faith.

Stepping out in faith requires that we open up our hearts and allow the Spirit of God and H<small>IS</small> Son to enter in and teach us the way home to our eternal life. This is your eternal invitation and it may be the only one you will ever receive in this life. Listen to God.

God Speaks

> **"Then those who feared the L<small>ORD</small> [God] spoke to one another, and the L<small>ORD</small> [God] listened and heard them; so, a book of remembrance was written before H<small>IM</small> for those who fear the L<small>ORD</small> and who meditate on H<small>IS</small> name. 'They shall be M<small>INE</small>, says the L<small>ORD</small> of hosts, on the day that I make them M<small>Y</small> jewels, and I will spare them as a man spares his own son who serves him.' Then you shall again discern between the righteous and the wicked, between one who serves God and one who does not serve H<small>IM</small>."**
>
> **Malachi 3:16-18**

> **"Salvation belongs to our God who sits on the throne, *and* to the Lamb [Jesus at the right hand of God]." Revelation 7:11**
>
> **Jesus said: "Most assuredly, I say to you, he who hears my word and believes in HIM [God, the FATHER] who sent me has everlasting life, and shall not come into judgment, but has [already] passed from death into [eternal] life." John 5:24**

If you know the God who sent Jesus, you already have eternal life and you will not be judged at the time of your death.

> **Jesus said: "And this is eternal life, that they may know YOU [God, the FATHER], the only true God, and Jesus Christ whom YOU have sent."**
> **John 17:3**
>
> **Jesus said: "My doctrine is not mine, but HIS [God, the FATHER] who sent me." John 7:16**

God has always wanted the best for your life. HIS invitation for an eternal life did not just start with Jesus. An expression of God's great love for you can be found in Ezekiel chapter 18. From the beginning of history you will find God hoping for our best and hoping we would turn away from wickedness and to a life of righteousness.

Righteousness brings us into fellowship with God. *That is when* we truly become HIS people for eternity.

It's a choice for God, in faith, knowing that we are just travelers here on a temporary earthly journey. Our big decision on earth will be to accept the reality that God exists and that life truly transcends this existence. Knowing in our hearts that as Jesus was resurrected, so will God resurrect us.

> **"Do not love the world or the things in the world. If anyone loves the world, the love of the FATHER is not in him." 1 John 2:15**

> **Jesus said: "It is the Spirit who gives life; the flesh profits nothing. The words that I speak to you are spirit, and they are life." John 6:63**

I am the Apostle Edward. I write to reach souls with God's invitation of an eternal life. However, I especially write to those souls who claim salvation through Christ, but have been misled to think that Christ is God.

Many Christians do not know the God that Christ served. If this is you, your eternal life is in question. You need to get right with God and reject the Church apostasy that has people now praying to and worshipping Jesus instead of the God that Jesus himself served and taught us about. Anyone who worships the Son of God as "God the Son" commits idolatry in God's eyes. Such people are not truly saved, but instead are in "spiritual hot water." Worship of Jesus is the same as worshipping any Priest or Pastor. God has said to have no other god's besides HIM. That includes HIS Son.

Study the Scriptures cited in this chapter [*The Invitation*] very carefully. While in the Spirit, God gave these Scriptures to me for your benefit. That applies to virtually every other chapter in this book as well. Please open up your heart to God's Word and let Jesus Christ, our Teacher, become the example you follow all the way back to your own heavenly home.

Do this and you will not only love Jesus and the sacrifice he made for our sins on the cross, you will also fall in love with God. You can call HIM heavenly FATHER in all of your prayers.

Apostle's Prayer

Heavenly FATHER and God of my brother Jesus Christ, who is our Teacher, hear my prayer. Bless every soul that reads this chapter and will open up their heart to YOUR Son Jesus and also to YOUR Spirit. And, to all who pray the prayer below and accept your invitation, grant them repentance. Edward

Prayer To Accept God's Invitation

FATHER God, I accept this special invitation of YOURS to an eternal life in heaven.

I confess with my mouth that YOU raised Jesus Christ from the dead and that he is the first of many humans to be resurrected to be with YOU, as YOUR sons and daughters.

I believe in my heart unto righteousness and I will do my best to live a righteous life in YOUR eyes. I will follow the example of Jesus and be faithful unto my own death.

FATHER, I thank you that YOU and YOUR Son will become one with me to help me overcome this earthly life. I know that this will make us of one mind and that YOUR Spirit will dwell within me to guide my path back home. Teach me YOUR ways LORD.

Date _____ _____
                                  Signature

The Apostle Edward

Please accept God's Invitation to an eternal life. This may be the only time you will be presented with God's Word. These are only the basics, but they will get you started on a life with God and HIS human begotten Son, Jesus Christ.

You must understand that Jesus Christ is God's human begotten Son; he is not God. It is as simple as believing what Jesus taught us and accepting Scripture over manmade church doctrine.

If your church doesn't preach God's Word, find another church that does. You can read more about this topic and others contained in this book online at the following link http://www.bookofedward.org. You can also sign up for a free newsletter and read my blog at this link. May God bless you!

Notations in small caps such as LORD, HE, HIM, HIS, YOU, and FATHER refer to God and not to Jesus.

The Key To Unlock Scripture

If you keep the relationship between God and HIS begotten human Son Jesus Christ straight, you will understand your Holy Bible and God's invitation to an eternal life will be for real. This relationship is the key to successfully understanding God's Word. Do not try to interpret Scripture using the trinity doctrine; it makes Jesus a liar in such simple verses as John 20:17. It also makes Paul a liar in such simple verses as 1 Corinthians 8:6.

Two Heart Gateways

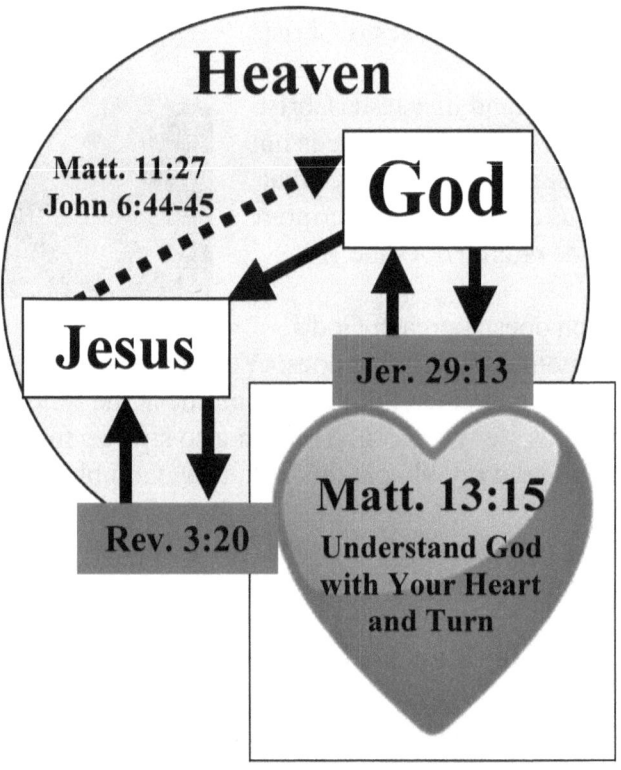

The Messenger

> In Jesus' parable of the Vineyard, the landowner represents God HIMSELF. The servants represent messengers sent by God. The son represents Jesus. The harvest of grapes represents souls. In this story from Jesus, all messengers of God, including God's only human begotten son, are killed. To fully understand God, you need to understand the fact that God sent HIS only begotten human son, Jesus Christ, as another "Messenger."
>
> **Apostle Edward**

Bible Verse: Matthew 21:33-40

The Messenger Contents

	Page
The Messenger	61
A Story About God's Son	63
When God Comes Back	63-64
There Is Only One God	64
Salvation Comes From God	65
A Pass For Eternal Life	65
A Last Day Pickup Plan	66-67
Jesus Identifies God	68
Last Day Pickup Graphic	68
One Group Is Not Judged	69
Everyone Else Is Judged	69
What Judges Us On Last Day	70
Ten Teachings Of Jesus	71-73
Spiritual Metaphors	73
The Lord Jesus Christ	74
Eternal Life Without God?	74-75

A Story About God's Son

Jesus said, "There was a man who owned a vineyard. He put a wall around it and dug a hole for a winepress and built a tower. Then he leased the land to some farmers and left for a trip. When it was time for the grapes to be picked, he sent his servants to the farmers to get his share of the grapes. But the farmers grabbed the servants, beat one, killed another, and then killed a third servant with stones. So the man sent some other servants to the farmers, even more than he sent the first time. But the farmers did the same thing to the servants that they had done before. So the man decided to send his son to the farmers. He said, 'They will respect my son.' But when the farmers saw the son, they said to each other, 'This son will inherit the vineyard. If we kill him, it will be ours!' Then the farmers grabbed the son, threw him out of the vineyard, and killed him. So what will the owner of the vineyard do to these farmers when he comes?"

Matthew 21:33-40 (NCV)

Jesus Tells Us God Comes Back

The verse above is from the New Century Bible. Christians often hear about the second coming of Jesus, but few realized that God HIMSELF also comes back. In the above story, Jesus indicates that God, the Vineyard owner, will come back. We also read that God comes back in Isaiah.

Isaiah Tells Us God Comes Back

> "Prepare the way of the LORD [GOD]; Make straight in the desert a highway for our God...
>
> The glory of the LORD shall be revealed, and all flesh shall see it together;
>
> For the mouth of the LORD has spoken."
>
> Isaiah 40:3-5

All humans [flesh] have not yet seen God's glory together, so this event is yet to occur.

There Is Only One God

> " 'You are MY witnesses,' says the LORD, And MY servant whom I have chosen, that you may know and believe ME, and understand that I am HE. Before ME there was no God formed, nor shall there be after ME. I, *even* I, am the LORD, and besides ME [God] there is no SAVIOR."
>
> Isaiah 43:10-11

This verse may disturb some Christians who hold onto the false belief in a triune god and salvation only through the god Jesus. The Bible does not teach this lie; the orthodox Trinitarian and doctrinal church teaches it.

This chapter highlights some characteristics of Jesus Christ, "The Messenger" of God. It starts out by acknowledging that there is only one God who is SAVIOR of mankind. Jesus teaches that God granted him the ability to also provide salvation [Eternal Life].

Salvation Comes From God

> Jesus said: "For as the FATHER [God] has life [salvation] in HIMSELF, so HE [God] has granted the Son [Jesus] to [also] have life in himself."
> **John 5:26**

In the above words of Jesus, we learn that God has granted Jesus the ability to provide salvation to souls. So, while salvation only comes from God, HE has granted authority to Jesus to give eternal life to those souls who believe in him and obey his gospel. We also read this fact in the book of Revelation.

> "Salvation belongs to our God who sits on the throne, *and* to the Lamb [Christ who sits at the right hand of God]." **Revelation 7:10**

This means there are TWO PATHS to Eternal Life. One is directly from God and the other comes through faith in HIS only begotten human son Jesus.

A Pass For Eternal Life

If you read "The Invitation" – you already realize this reality of salvation. I repeat it here to reinforce the teaching of Jesus found in John, which reads as follows:

> Jesus said: "Most assuredly, I say to you, he who hears my word and believes in HIM who sent me has everlasting life, and shall not come into judgment, but has passed from death into life."
> **John 5:24**

It is Jesus who states the above reality of eternal life. IF you believe in the God who sent "The Messenger" Jesus, *you already have passed into eternal life and did so without any judgment.* So, what if you don't believe Jesus was sent as a messenger, but believe he is God? Well, Jesus gives us that answer. Jesus says he will pick you up on the "Last Day" for judgment.

A Last Day Pickup Plan

There is a difference "The Messenger" Jesus makes between believing in "the God who sent him" and in just believing in him. Have you heard about the *Last Day Pickup Plan*?

> **"I am the bread of life. He who comes to me shall never hunger, and he who believes in me shall never thirst. But I said to you that you have seen me and yet do not believe. All that the FATHER gives me will come to me, and the one who comes to me, I will by no means cast out. For I have come down from heaven, not to do my own will, but the will of HIM who sent me. This is the will of the FATHER [God] who sent me, that of all HE has given me I should lose nothing, but should raise it up on the last day." John 6:35-39**

Jesus offers us two very odd teachings on how to gain eternal life. First, you could believe in the God who sent Jesus and that he was a messenger [Son] in which case you get a "pass" into heaven that bypasses any judgment. Now, belief in this instance does imply adhering to God's ways & commands. In the second teaching, you just believe in Jesus and he will "raise you up on the last day." There is more about this last day pickup plan.

Here are some additional teachings of Jesus on God's *Last Day Pickup Plan*.

> **"This is the will of HIM who sent me, that everyone who sees the Son and believes in him may have everlasting life; and I will raise him up at the last day." John 6:40**
>
> **"No one can come to me unless the FATHER who sent me draws him [or her]; and I will raise him [or her] up at the last day." John 6:44**
>
> **Jesus said: "Whoever eats my flesh and drinks my blood has eternal life, and I will raise him [or her] up at the last day." John 6:54**

This last verse is, of course, only a metaphor. We do not literally eat flesh or drink blood. This statement means that we instead take on Jesus' burden to reach lost souls. We emulate Christ who becomes our teacher. By following Christ's example, we become obedient to God's commandments.

God showed me HIS "*Last Day Pickup Plan*" several years ago. However, it was only recently that God explained it to me in a way that I could fully understand. It was at my dear friend Vernon's funeral. As I sat there pondering my friend, who died at the age of 82, God spoke to my spirit clearly and indicated to me that John 5:24 applied to Vernon, because Vernon knew his God [Yahweh].

This is to say that Vernon knew who God was and he knew that Jesus was not God, but a messenger sent by God. Vernon knew and believed the teachings of Jesus in this regards. Vernon knew Jesus made it clear that he was just a messenger and a prophet sent by God. Vernon knew that Jesus identified God as our FATHER.

Jesus Identifies God

> **Jesus said: "I am ascending to my FATHER and your FATHER, and to my God and your God."**
> **John 20:17**

These are very simple words from Jesus. He speaks of the God that we all are to serve. Is it important to know God and that Jesus is not God, but was just a messenger? Yes, it is and the answer is found in 2 Thessalonians 1:8.

As I was leaving Vernon's funeral, I stopped to thank the friend who gave his eulogy. He was well versed in Scripture. I told him that John 5:24 applied to Vernon. That Vernon had passed into heaven without judgment. Then I heard a strange reply.

He replied: "Of course, all Christians are not judged." It was God's way of showing me the apostasy and lack of understanding of HIS Son within Christianity at large. I let it go, because a funeral is not a time to debate anyone about God's Holy Word.

The eulogist's statement that all Christians are not judged was his Church indoctrination and Church dogma and not the word of God. Graphically, we see Jesus has taught us this.

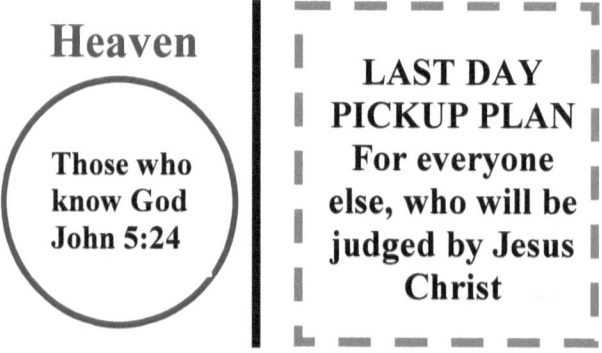

One Group Is Not Judged

*In the teachings of Jesus, only **one group gets a pass** into "everlasting life, and shall not come into judgment."*

It is not my words but the words of Jesus in John 5:24. This group represents all people who know God and are righteous in HIS eyes. This could include people who do not know Jesus or for that matter may not know much about Jesus.

In contrast, everyone who knows Jesus, but does not know the God that sent him will be "picked up at the last day" for judgment. Why are Christians judged? Well, not all will be. However, Jesus makes it clear that many who call upon him will not get into heaven. He states this clearly in Matthew 7:21-23. Jesus also gives us the reason. Those who he rejects as never having known were "lawless." They did not obey God. In essence, they never got to know who God actually was. And, that HE is a righteous God that values righteousness in HIS people.

Everyone Else Is Judged

Jesus Christ will pick you up on the last day if you do not know God Almighty, ***the God who sent Jesus***. This "last day" refers to the Day of Judgment. If you die before this last day occurs, your soul will go into a holding place until that time occurs. This is what I believe at this time. I know that Jesus has taught us that those who know his God, "has everlasting life and shall not come into judgment, but has passed from death into life." Is this you? Do you really know God? The God that Jesus served? The God that Jesus identified in John 20:17? Or, do you think Jesus is God?

What Judges Us On Last Day

In John 12, Jesus tells us what will judge those who are picked up on the last day. Jesus says, "It's the word that I have spoken." Since Jesus spoke as a prophet and only the words he received from God, it will be God's Word that will judge everyone picked up on the last day.

Those who believe in Jesus are also picked up on the last day, so God's Word will also judge them. This certainly represents everyone who believes in the Church man-made trinity doctrine. Why? It's because they never believed Jesus when he taught them who God was in John 20:17. Those who know that *God is only the FATHER and is YAHWEH, the God of the Jews,* are covered under the teaching of Jesus in John 5:24. Remember? They get a pass!

> **"He who rejects me, and does not receive my words, has that which judges him [or her]—the word [from God] that I have spoken will judge him [or her] in the last day." John 12:48-39**

Jesus' words [given to him by God] will judge everyone picked up on the last day. Can you see from the above teachings of Jesus that the Church has altered God's message that Jesus brought to us 2,000 years ago? It is Jesus who taught us he spoke God's words.

> **Jesus said: "He who does not love me does not keep my words; and the word which you hear is not mine, but the FATHER'S [God's] who sent me." John 14:24**

Let's examine some more characteristics of "The Messenger" Jesus, from his own words and teachings found in the Bible.

Ten Teachings Of Jesus

1. **God sent Jesus.**

    a. Matthew 10:40; 15:24
    b. Luke 4:18; 4:43; 9:48
    c. John 4:30; 5:24, 30, 36, 37, 38;
    John 6:29, 38, 39, 40, 44
    John 7:16, 18, 28, 29, 30
    John 8:16, 18, 26, 29, 42
    John 9:4; 10:26; 11:42; 12:44, 45
    John 12:49; 13:16, 20; 14:24
    John 15:21; 16:5; 17:3, 8, 18, 21
    John 17:25; 20:21
    Acts 3:26

2. **God gave Jesus a purpose.**

    a. Jesus said: "I must preach the kingdom of God to the other cities also, because for this purpose I have been sent [by God]." Luke 4:43

3. **Jesus only did the will of God.**

    a. Jesus said: "My food is to do the will of HIM who sent me, and to finish HIS work." John 4:34

4. **Jesus did nothing on his own accord.**

    a. Jesus said: "I can of myself do nothing. As I hear, I judge; and my judgment is righteous, because I do not seek my own will but the will of the FATHER who sent me." John 5:30

5. **Jesus came from Heaven to do God's will.**
    a. Jesus said: "For I have come down from heaven, not to do my own will, but the will of HIM [God] who sent me."
    John 6:38

6. **Jesus must perform the works of God.**
    a. Jesus said: "I must work the works of HIM who sent me while it is day, the night is coming when no one can work."
    John 9:4

7. **Jesus' doctrine was God's, not his.**
    a. Jesus said: "My doctrine is not mine, but HIS who sent me." John 7:16

8. **God was greater than Jesus was.**
    a. Jesus said: "If you loved me, you would rejoice because I said, 'I am going to my FATHER,' for my FATHER is greater than I [am]" John 14:28. *See John 13:16 also.*

9. **Jesus spoke God's Words, not his own.**
    a. Jesus said: "He who does not love me does not keep my words; and the word which you hear is not mine, but the FATHER'S [God's] who sent me."
    John 14:24

10. **Eternal life was to know Jesus' God.**
    a. Jesus said: "And this is eternal life, that they may know YOU [God], the only true God, and Jesus Christ whom YOU have sent." John 17:3

Of course, Jesus taught many other things, but you cannot understand any of Jesus' teachings unless you understand first that he was not God, but a messenger of God sent to give our souls another opportunity for eternal life.

Jesus left this earth more than just a great messenger of God. He also gave up his own human life as a perfect sacrifice for our sins.

Spiritual Metaphors

In many teachings, Jesus spoke in spiritual metaphors. To understand such teachings, you have to use your spirit instead of your physical senses or mental facilities. Ergo, think spiritually!

When Jesus said in John 12:45: **"He who sees me sees HIM who sent me"** – Jesus used a spiritual metaphor. Jesus was telling us that if we really saw who he was "with our spiritual eyes" that we could see God HIMSELF spiritually from within Jesus.

Thus, if we engage our spirit, having been born again of the Spirit and the living word inside of us, as Peter taught, we see clearly that God *sent* Jesus. Another key to understanding a true believer in Jesus is given in this verse.

> **Jesus said: "He who believes in me, believes not in me but in HIM who sent me." John 12:44**

Jesus states you would believe in the God who *sent him* IF you really believed. Peter taught us that we will have placed our "faith and hope in God" alone as a result of having known Jesus and through Jesus having returned back to God. See 1 Peter 1:21-22. Ergo, true belief in Jesus leads you back to his God [YAHWEH]!

Think about it!

The Lord Jesus Christ

The story of our Lord Jesus Christ is a very compelling one. God sent HIS only human begotten Son as a perfect sacrifice for the sins of mankind. It was God reconciling mankind so HIS need for perfect justice could be satisfied. Jesus' human sacrifice became not only the atonement for the sins of mankind, but also our human example to follow even unto our own death.

Jesus taught us to worship only the LORD God who sent him. He would be greatly disturbed by all of the churches that now worship him instead of his God. Jesus taught us to worship his God in Matthew 4:10 and in other verses.

If you want Eternal Life, get to know the God that sent Jesus as "The Messenger." Only then will you have truly received the message of our Lord Jesus Christ.

Eternal Life Without God?

If you are an astute student of the Bible, this discussion of "The Messenger" may have raised more questions for you than it gave you answers. This is good. It will help you bring out the truth by studying God's Word, especially the Scriptures cited.

Could there be any salvation or eternal life without actually coming to know God and not just Jesus? Let's put it this way. Do you believe you can mouth Jesus as your savior and get into Heaven? Or is there more to it?

> **"And having been perfected, [Jesus] became the author of eternal salvation to all who OBEY him [and obey his God, the FATHER]." Hebrews 5:9**

If you haven't found the God who *sent* Jesus, claims of faith in Jesus are most likely unfounded. Jesus calls us to obey his God!

Study the Scriptures cited in this chapter very carefully. While in the Spirit, God gave these Scriptures to me for your benefit.

Please open up your heart to God's Word and let Jesus Christ, our Teacher, become the example you follow all the way back to your own heavenly home.

Do this and you will not only love Jesus and the sacrifice he made for our sins, you will also fall in love with God. You can call HIM heavenly FATHER in all of your prayers.

Apostle's Prayer

Heavenly FATHER and God of my brother Jesus Christ, who is our Teacher, hear my prayer. Bless every soul that reads this chapter and will open up their heart to YOUR human begotten Son, Jesus Christ, and also to YOUR Spirit. And, to all who pray the salvation prayer accepting your invitation at the end of The Invitation or prays the more comprehensive salvation prayer in Appendix A, at the end of this book, grant them repentance. Edward

The Message

> **Jesus said: "Seeing they do not see, and hearing they do not hear, nor do they understand." Many say Jesus is your only way to get to heaven. Yet, this is not what Jesus taught. My mind is open to God and HIS truth, so I listen when God speaks. Hearing HIM, I understand. My eyes are open to God so when I read the Bible, I perceive God and HE speaks to me through HIS Word. What about you? Are your ears, eyes and mind open to God's message? Or, do these words of Jesus in Matthew apply to you?**
>
> Apostle Edward

Bible Verse: Matthew 13:13

The Message Contents

	Page
The Message	77
Spiritual Communications	79
Go Directly To God	79-80
Enter The Holiest	80
Reticular Activating System	81-82
The Bereans Tested Paul	83-84
Have You Received The Love Of The Truth?	84
Matthew 13:10-19	85
Parable Of The Sower	86
The Four Receivers Of God's Word	87
The Truth Of Scripture	87-89
Don't Forget Free Will	90
John 14:6 Exegesis	90-91
Four Salvation Truths	92
More Salvation Truths	92-94
YAHWEH is the God Jesus Served	94-96
What did Jesus Say?	96-97
Peter Sums Up *The Message*	97

Spiritual Communications

In "The Messenger", you learned that Jesus often spoke to his disciples using spiritual metaphors.

> **"It is the Spirit who gives life, the flesh profits nothing. The words that I speak to you are spirit, and they are life. But there are some of you who do not believe." John 6:63-64**

Did people gasp for air when Jesus said they had to eat his flesh and drink his blood? Jesus went on to clarify that he was only talking in spiritual terms. Jesus used "spirit words" and a spiritual metaphor. Keep this in mind as you seek to understand the Bible. Jesus also said:

> **"In that day you will ask me nothing. Most assuredly, I say to you, whatever you ask the FATHER in my name HE will give you."**
> **John 16:23-24**

Go Directly To God

Speaking with God used to be a restricted affair. Only the High Priest was allowed. However, Christ changed all of that and taught us to "go direct" to our FATHER [God] with our prayers and petitions. Jesus also said we would no longer have any need to ask of him *for anything*.

> **"And in that day you will ask me nothing. Most assuredly, I say to you, whatever you ask the FATHER in my name HE will give you." John 16:24**

The New Living Translation (NLT) is as follows:

> **Jesus said: "At the time [when I leave], you won't need to ask me for anything. The truth is, you can go directly to the FATHER and ask HIM, and HE will grant your request because you use my name." John 16:23-24 (NLT)**

Jesus destroyed all of the religious restrictions when it comes to communicating with God. Jesus also gave us the ability to go into God's Holy of Holies if we have given our hearts to God. Ergo, you do not need a priest, a bishop, a cardinal or a pope to talk directly with God. IF you've truly accepted Christ, the Holy Spirit will reside in you and give you the courage to go directly to God.

Enter The Holiest

> **"Therefore, brethren, having boldness to enter the Holiest [of Holies] by the blood of Jesus, by a new and living way ... [to talk directly with our God and Heavenly FATHER]." Hebrews 9:19-20**

Those who have accepted the sacrifice of God's only human begotten Son, Jesus, and who have received the teachings of Jesus, have returned back to God Almighty. They now communicate directly with God and they ask of God in Jesus' name to honor Jesus. God's people can now enter into HIS Holy of Holies to fellowship with God at any time they desire, day or night.

To understand "The Message", you must have fully surrendered your heart to God as I discussed in "The Invitation" and in "The Messenger." Having done that, your ears, eyes and mind are now fully open to God and HIS ways. You are obedient to the teachings of Christ. You are now a slave to righteousness, to God's ways.

Reticular Activating System

Only when your mind is fully open, can you understand that Christ destroyed all religious systems. Given this fact, you are free to go directly to God without having to go through a religious organization that seeks to control or limit your access to God. I would add that since Christ's death, the organized religious Church has reestablished itself with various orthodox doctrines for the explicit purpose of controlling God's people. **Caution ...**

Your church should be a place to learn God's Word. It should also be a place of fellowship, support and, above all, a place of worship and prayer. You may find that a home church as described in the New Testament is the best. In a home church, everyone provides inputs and thoughts and together discern God's Word. Interactive, spiritually dynamic, small group Bible study replaces one-way sermons and the typical doctrinal programming found in churches.

IF you belong to a big church, you should participate in a small Bible study group to make sure you grow in God's Word. Then, there is our "Reticular Activating System."

IF you have not had your mind opened as I have described, it may be because it is either partially or fully shut down by your Reticular Activating System or RAS. God provided us with an information gatekeeper in our minds to help us manage our information intake.

The RAS is located in our brain stem and is used to either accept or reject ideas and input. Ideas and inputs are automatically accepted or ignored as affirming or conflicting with a prior held belief. The RAS operates on the level of the subconscious, but we consciously control it.

If we have an idea or belief that we hold as absolutely solid, then the RAS automatically rejects anything that conflicts with that belief. Conversely, it allows in anything affirming it.

Ideas come from many different sources into our brains. Some of them become like seeds in the garden called our belief system. Belief seeds planted into our minds grow stronger when they gain a root structure containing references that support the belief. A strongly held belief has deep reference roots that may include people or even a pastor or a church you have come to respect over many years; perhaps a church you've attended over four decades.

Belief roots can include a family history of supporting one religion over another. The root structure can also become strong as the result of repeated mental programming.

Once ingrained into our minds, such strong beliefs are managed subconsciously by our RAS. It is because our brains have a limited amount of mental real estate we are willing to devote to different issues. The RAS, as a gatekeeper, reinforces what we believe is true and rejects what we believe are lies. Yet, each one of us decides what we believe.

As an adult, many will have to challenge the beliefs passed down from our parents and prior generations. I myself have asked the question: "How did I come to believe this or that was true?" If you are still with me and I haven't lost you, these words from God may have a poignant meaning.

> **God said HE visits "the iniquity [sins] of the fathers upon the children to the third and the fourth generation." Exodus 34:7**

Parents, families, friends, schools, churches and various fellowship groups will pass down beliefs that are corrupt.

God holds each one of us accountable to discern truth. However, if you never challenge your beliefs, how do you know they are true?

As a Christian, you must test your teachers and discern whether what you are being taught lines up with the word of God. This is how you will come to know what truth is.

The Bereans Tested Paul

> **[The Bereans] "Were more fair-minded than those in Thessalonica, in that they received the word [of God] with all readiness, and searched the Scriptures [O.T.] daily to find out whether these things were so." Acts 17:11**

The people of Berea opened their minds to the Apostle Paul's teachings. However, they THEN searched Scriptures daily to verify that what Paul taught them was God's truth.

This is your test of a teacher of God's Word. That they teach Scripture in context and that you can verify their teachings with your own eyes. When the Bereans searched Scripture, it was the Old Testament. References in the New Testament to Scripture all refer to the Old Testament. You cannot understand the New Testament if you do not understand the Old Testament. And at all times you must stay within the contextual meaning of Scripture.

Are you starting to get a picture? *"Seeing they do not see, and hearing they do not hear, nor do they understand!"* Could it be that the people Jesus tried to teach were so programmed by an existing religious culture that their minds just automatically rejected any attempt by Jesus to impart God's Word? Yes, that could have been one explanation.

TODAY, we face a similar situation. For two thousand years, the Orthodox Church has programmed people with doctrines that are not supported by the word of God found in the Holy Bible.

Some Christians now have a difficult time trying to understand very simple Scripture. Why? Their minds have shut down dialog. Only when you love the truth are you able to reopen or examine an ingrained belief of the mind. The Apostle Paul warned us that we would perish if we did not love the truth.

> **"The coming of the lawless one is according to the working of Satan, with all power, signs, and lying wonders, and with all unrighteous deception among those who perish, because they did not receive the love of the truth, that they might be saved." 2 Thessalonians 2:9-10**

Have You Received The Love Of The Truth?

If you have truly given your whole heart to God, either by finding HIM directly or by finding God through HIS begotten human Son Jesus -- THEN you will have received the love of the truth. Without being a lover of the truth, you will have no eternal life.

You know you are a lover of the truth by exhibiting one attribute of your faith. What is that attribute? It's a love for God's Word.

You love God's Word more than anything else in life. More than your parents, spouse, children, friends, pastor and church. You love God's Word more than anything and anyone. And, if you find anyone's teachings in opposition to God's Word, you bring that Scripture to that person's attention.

Matthew 13:10-19

And the disciples came and said to [Jesus], "Why do you speak to [these people] in parables?" [Jesus] answered and said to them, "Because it has been given to you [disciples] to know the mysteries of the kingdom of heaven, but to them it has not been given. For whoever has, to him more will be given, and he will have abundance; but whoever does not have, even what he has will be taken away from him [or her].

Therefore I speak to [these people] in parables, because seeing they do not see, and hearing they do not hear, nor do they understand.

And in them the prophecy of Isaiah is fulfilled, which says: 'Hearing you will hear and shall not understand, and seeing you will see and not perceive; for the hearts of this people have grown dull.

Their ears are hard of hearing, and their eyes they have closed, lest they should see with their eyes and hear with their ears,

Lest they should understand with their hearts and turn, so that [God] should heal them.'

But blessed are your eyes for they see, and your ears for they hear; for assuredly, I say to you that many prophets and righteous men desired to see what you see, and did not see it, and to hear what you hear, and did not hear it." **Matthew 13:10-19**

Are your ears, eyes and mind now open?

It is important for your understanding of God's Word that your ears, eyes, and mind are now fully open to God. I want you to understand God's Word and to be fruitful for HIM. Listen to this...

Parable of the Sower

"Therefore hear parable of the sower: When anyone hears the word of the kingdom, and does not understand it, then the wicked one comes and snatches away what was sown in his heart. This is he who received [God's Word] by the wayside." Matthew 13:20

"But he who received the seed on stony places, this is he who hears the word and immediately receives it with joy; yet he has no root in himself, but endures only for a while. For when tribulation or persecution arises because of the word, immediately he stumbles." Matthew 13:20-21

"Now he who received the seed among the thorns is he who hears the word, and the cares of this world and the deceitfulness of riches choke the word, and he becomes unfruitful." Matthew 13:22

"But he [or she] who received the seed on good ground is he [or she] who hears the word and understands it, who indeed bears fruit and produces: some a hundredfold, some sixty, some thirty." Matthew 13:23

The Four Receivers Of God's Word

1. **Those who do not understand** will have the Word taken [or reasoned] away.

2. **Those who suffer trouble** *because of the Word* will stumble [and stop listening].

3. **Those concerned about the cares of this world and riches** will become unfruitful and will have the Word rendered useless.

4. **Those who understand** the Word will become fruitful servants of God.

Which category do you fall into as you hear God's Word? Will someone take the Word away from you? Will you stop listening? Will the Word become useless to you? Or, will you understand the Word and become a fruitful servant of God?

The Truth Of Scripture

Before the above teaching, Jesus had said in Matthew 11:15 and in Matthew 13:9 the following:

"He who has ears to hear let him H<small>EAR</small>!"

I tell you the same thing, right now! I am about to share some teachings of Jesus that may conflict with what you strongly believe is absolute truth. These may be strongly held beliefs in your mind reinforced by years and maybe decades of Church orthodox programming. Can you accept the simple truth of God's Word?

Think you can accept truth? If so, then let's start with Jesus' statement about returning to his God *and our God*.

> **Jesus said to her, "Do not cling to me, for I have not yet ascended to my FATHER; but go to my brethren and say to them, 'I am ascending to my FATHER and your FATHER, and <u>to my God</u> and your God.' " John 20:17**

The unambiguous and clear meaning of John 20:17 is that Jesus states that he has a God he is returning to. Jesus identifies his God as the FATHER. Jesus states clearly that his God is also our God and also our FATHER.

Do you acknowledge that Jesus had a God?

If not, stop here. This chapter seeks to impart Scriptural truth to you, but it is meaningless if you mentally cannot accept the simple language of Scripture. If you cannot acknowledge mentally that Jesus had a God from his very own teachings, it means that your mind is programmed with a strong orthodox trinity belief. It means that your RAS may be automatically rejecting any information that contradicts those orthodox teachings. It also means that you are not saved, because you reject and cannot accept this simple truth from Jesus found in Scripture. In 100% of all bibles, you will find the very same language from Jesus. Before going on, you will need to surrender your whole heart to God and HIS Word. Pray about it!

The words in John 20:17 are easily understood, but I have found that many orthodox Christians are "programmed" and unable to digest its simple truth. Instead, this verse leaves them with a blank stare in their eyes and causes them to shut down mentally and to then reject all further attempts at communications. For me, it is like showing the "Tithe Law" in Deuteronomy 14:22-29 to a Christian programmed to tithe to their church. Ergo, you get the same blank stare and mental shutdown. It's the RAS at work in our brains.

Let's try one more verse before getting into some Scriptures on salvation, including some things Jesus had to say about salvation.

> **"Therefore, in all things [Jesus] had to be MADE like his brethren [other humans], that he might be a merciful and faithful High Priest in things pertaining to God, to make propitiation for the sins of the people. For that [since] he himself has suffered, being tempted, he [Jesus] is able to aid those who are tempted." Hebrews 2:17-18**

Hebrews 2:17-18 Raises Questions

1. Do you believe Jesus was **MADE** just like us?
2. Do you believe Jesus is God's High Priest?
3. Do you believe Jesus was a male human like all males?
4. Do you believe Jesus suffered temptation like all humans?

These four attributes of Christ cannot be applied to God. They could be applied to another human, but the High Priest attribute is because God chose Christ for that role. Christ wasn't chosen to be "God the Son." That is an attribute the Church assigns to Jesus.

In *The Invitation* and *The Messenger* you were presented with similar Scriptures, which directly contradicted Orthodox Church teachings. So, fundamentally, you have a serious choice to make. Exactly whom will you choose to believe? Who is lying to us? Someone is! Is it the Church? God's Word? Jesus? Who?

The idea that somehow Jesus was both man and God is facetious on its face. Even worse though are the clear teachings from God's Word that speak directly against such a lie. If you want to study more about why the trinity doctrine is simply Church dogma, go to http://www.trinitydogma.com and get a copy of *Trinity Dogma*.

Don't Forget Free Will

I won't lose any sleep over people rejecting God's Word. I understand that not everyone is supposed to receive God's Word. Not everyone is headed to Heaven. Listen, we are NOT called to forcibly change people.

Which brings me to this final thought before actually moving into some Scriptures about salvation: "The Message" from God. Many believe that you must mentally beat people into accepting Jesus or that they will be lost to Hell. However, all God asks is to simply present HIS Word and let the people choose. To *respect* the free will God gave all people.

> **"He who is unjust, let him be unjust still; he who is filthy, let him be filthy still; he who is righteous, let him be righteous still; he who is holy, let him be holy still." Revelation 22:11**

John 14:6 Exegesis

> **Jesus said to him, "I am the way, the truth, and the life. No one comes to the FATHER except *through* me." John 14:6**

The Church has long held John 14:6 as proof there is no eternal life or salvation unless you accept Jesus as savior. However, if this were true, there would be no Bible verses contradicting such a doctrine.

The explanation for this verse is simpler. Jesus spoke and did what God told him to say and do. Jesus said that if you believed in him, you really believed in the God who sent him.

Ergo, "The way, the truth, and the life" refer to God's Word. It is God's Word that leads you home to Heaven. The phrase "no one comes to the FATHER except *through* me" literally reflects the fact that heaven's judgment line forms to the right of Jesus.

Since Christ will judge souls for God and he sits at God's right hand, and the judgment line forms to the right of Christ – *It means that every soul will literally go through or by Christ before they get to the FATHER.*

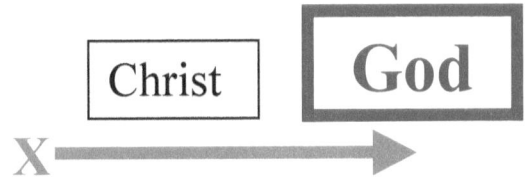

Judgment line starts at "X" to the left of Christ as you face the throne of God!

John 14:6 is that easy to understand. While this exegesis may be unsettling to some, it does not require that you check your brain in at the front door of the church and ignore many Scripture verses that oppose the Orthodox interpretation of the verse.

In Malachi 3:6 God says, "For I am the LORD, I do not change." With that in mind, fully consider Ezekiel 18 in which God gives us the criteria HE uses for salvation. Nothing has changed in the criteria God has established. It is a repentant heart and a righteous lifestyle. Christ confirms this in the New Testament. So, to claim John 14:6 means Jesus is the *only way,* literally makes God a liar in Ezekiel chapter 18. Also, calling on God [Yahweh] leads to salvation in Joel 2:32. It isn't the Word that lies; it is the Church!

Let me point out a few other Scriptures to consider. A detailed discussion of this subject is also found in the *Book of Edward*.

Four Salvation Truths

1. YAHWEH [God Almighty] said: "Before ME there was no God formed, nor shall there be after ME. I *even* I, am the LORD, and besides ME there is no SAVIOR." Isaiah 43:10-11

2. Jesus said: "For as the FATHER [God] has life [salvation] in HIMSELF, so HE [God] has granted the Son [Jesus] to have life in himself." John 5:26

3. "Salvation belongs to our God who sits on the throne, *and* to the Lamb [Christ who sits at the right hand of God]." Revelation 7:10

4. "Having been *born again*, not of corruptible seed but incorruptible, *through the Word of God*, which lives and abides forever."
   1 Peter 1:23

These four Scriptures and many others refute the idea that there is no salvation outside of Jesus. Such teachings reflect ignorance of God's Holy Word.

More Salvation Truths

1. King David said salvation belongs to YAHWEH. Psalms 3:8

2. Apostle John said salvation belongs to YAHWEH. Revelation 7:10

3. Jesus said salvation belongs to YAHWEH in John 5:26.

4. YAHWEH said that whoever praises HIM has salvation. Psalms 50:23

5. YAHWEH said that whoever orders his conduct aright has salvation. Psalms 50:23

6. Jesus said that whoever believes in YAHWEH has salvation. John 5:24

7. YAHWEH said that whoever calls on HIM has salvation. Joel 2:32

8. Paul said we believe with our hearts unto righteousness [salvation]. Romans 10:10

9. Hebrews teaches that whoever obeys Jesus' teachings has salvation. Hebrews 5:9

10. Paul said that whoever is awake to righteousness has salvation. 1 Corinthians 15:34

11. Paul said whoever does not sin has salvation. Romans 4:8

12. Paul said whoever is set free from sin has salvation. Romans 6:22

13. John said that whoever believes in Jesus and believes what Jesus taught has salvation.
John 3:16, 3:36

14. YAHWEH said whoever is faithful to HIM has salvation. Ezekiel 18:9

15. YAHWEH said whoever turns away from wickedness has salvation. Ezekiel 18:21

16. YAHWEH said whoever gets a new heart has salvation. Ezekiel 18:31

17. YAHWEH said righteous people, will see HIS salvation. Ezekiel 14:14

18. Jesus said benefactors of an apostle's forgiveness have salvation. John 20:23

19. Jesus said those who obey the Ten Commandments of God have salvation. Matthew 19:17

20. Jesus said a minimum righteousness level means salvation. Matthew 5:20

21. Solomon said righteous people would see salvation. Wisdom 5:2

22. Jesus said righteous people would see salvation. Matthew 13:43

YAHWEH is the God Jesus served!

Given the above teachings from the Bible regarding salvation, Jesus is not the only way to heaven. It is obvious God had much more in HIS mind when it comes to granting humans eternal life or what we now call salvation, even if it is granted through our belief in Jesus Christ as our Lord and savior. Yes, there are some strings attached to our behavior on this earth and it's not simply a matter of mouthing Jesus as our Lord.

Jesus rejects some Christians who claim him [and mouth him] as their Lord. Therefore, even Jesus says there is more to salvation than just claiming him as Lord, savior and master of our lives. It's obedience to God's Word!

> **Jesus said: "Not everyone who says to me, 'Lord, Lord' shall enter the kingdom of heaven, but he or she who does the will of my FATHER in heaven." Matthew 7:21**

So, we can see that "calling on the name of Jesus" is not a guarantee of salvation. One of the reasons for the confusion in Christianity is a misinterpretation of Apostle Paul in Romans.

> **For "whoever calls upon the name of the LORD shall be saved." Romans 10:13**

The word LORD in this verse, when properly translated refers to YAHWEH or God. And, Paul is actually citing Scripture from Joel. Paul is not stating that you can call on the name of Jesus and you "shall be saved."

> **"And it shall come to pass that whoever calls on the name of the LORD, shall be saved." Joel 2:32**

Jesus confirms that those who believe in YAHWEH or "the God who sent him" *have* passed from death into life in John 5:24. It is these people who **"shall be saved."** This is consistent with the *last day pickup plan* of God disclosed in *The Messenger* chapter.

> **"He [or she] who practices righteousness is righteous, just as [Jesus] is righteous."**
> **1 John 3:7**

Real faith leads us into a love affair with the God Jesus served. We then strive to obey God's Word and to emulate Jesus. This doesn't make us perfect, but it means we *do* practice God's righteousness.

What Did Jesus Say?

> **"From that time Jesus began to preach and to say, 'Repent, for the kingdom of heaven is at hand.' " Matthew 4:17**

> **Jesus said: "I did not come to call the righteous, but sinners, to repentance." Matthew 9:13**

The Gospel of Jesus was not to mouth him as savior. The Gospel of Jesus was *"repent, for the kingdom of heaven is at hand."* And what about those who received John's water baptism for repentance and the remission of their sins. Are they saved? Eternal life?

Jesus clearly states that those who received John's water baptism will enter the kingdom.

> **"I say to you that tax collectors and harlots *enter the kingdom of God before you*. For John came to you in the way of righteousness, and you did not believe him, but tax collectors and harlots believed him and when you saw it, you did not afterward relent and believe [John]."**
> **Matthew 21:31-32**

Is this a problem for the doctrinal church? It should be. Here we have the situation where Jesus wasn't even involved. However, even though the people did not receive Jesus, they repented to God and received John's water baptism for the remission of their sins.

> Jesus said: "Unless you repent you will all likewise perish." Luke 13:3

> *Repentance will get you home to Heaven!*

Many preach that righteous people do not exist, but this is also ignorance of God's Word.

> "And [Zacharias and Elizabeth] were both righteous before God, walking in all the commandments and ordinances of the LORD blameless." Luke 1:6

Peter Sums Up *The Message*!

Peter sums up "The Message" that God wanted you to hear. Open your heart to the word of God and accept this teaching of Peter.

> **Then Peter said to them, "Repent, and let every one of you be baptized in the name of Jesus Christ for the remission of sins; and you shall receive the gift of the Holy Spirit. For the promise is to you and to your children, and to all who are afar off, as many as the LORD our God will call." Acts 2:38-39**

> *Repent and be baptized in the name of Jesus!*

This is The Message!

Law of Christ

> **Many Christian teachers claim that the Apostle Paul taught God's Law no longer applies to Christians. They claim that salvation is all about God's Grace ever since Jesus was crucified on the cross. Yet Apostle Paul taught us this: "To those without [or outside the] law I became as one without law, not that I am without the law of God and lawless toward HIM, but that I am [especially keeping] within and committed to the law of Christ, that I might win whose who are without law."**
>
> Apostle Edward

Bible Reference: 1 Corinthians 9:21

Law of Christ Contents

	Page
Law Of Christ	99
I am <u>Not</u> Lawless!	101-102
Paul Said: I Obey The Law of Christ	102-103
The Nicolaitans	103-104
A Modern Baptist	104-105
I <u>Serve</u> The Law of God	105
You <u>Can</u> Obey God	106-108
A Sabbath Day Teaching	108-109
Teach The Law	109-110
Summation Of The Law	110-111
Summation Of Sin	111-112
God's Internal Program	112-113
It's Really About Righteousness	113-115
Locked Out Of Heaven	115
Christ's Higher Standard	116-119
Show People God's Love Inside Of You	119

I am <u>Not</u> Lawless!

Paul says: "I am not lawless." His statement in 1 Corinthians 9:21 is straightforward, simple, and sounds mild. One does not detect a lot of emotion in Paul's words. Yet, wouldn't Paul be mad today and screaming it out loud in anger? Because of those who now twist his words and say God's Law is done away with completely? The verse on the cover page of this chapter is from the Amplified Bible. The King James Bible (KJV) and New International (NIV) read as follows:

> **"To them that are under the law, [I became] as under the law; to them that are without law, as without law, (being not without law to God, but under the law to Christ), that I might gain them that are without law."**
> **1 Corinthians 9:20-21 (KJV)**

> **"I am not free from God's Law but am under Christ's Law." 1 Corinthians 9:21 (NIV)**

The New Living Translation (NLT) reads:

> **"When I am with the Jews, I become one of them so that I can bring them to Christ. When I am with those who follow the Jewish laws, I do the same, even though I am not subject to the [Jewish] law, so that I can bring them to Christ. When I am with the Gentiles who do not have the Jewish law, I fit in with them as much as I can. In this way, I gain their confidence and bring them to Christ. But I do not discard the law of God; I obey the law of Christ."**
> **1 Corinthians 9:20-21 (NLT)**

Get the picture? Paul was not lawless, was he? No! While Paul tried to fit in with any people that he found himself with, he did not "discard" God's Law. However, Paul stated something new, didn't he? He added the phrase "I obey the law of Christ." So what does it mean to obey the law of Christ?

This is the main question that is answered in this chapter. Two related questions will also be answered. These are: (1) Are God's Laws done away with? And, (2) what is the difference between the "Law of God" and the "Law of Christ?"

Before going on, let me make it very clear exactly what Paul has said in 1 Corinthians 9:21.

Paul Said: "I am <u>Not</u> Lawless; I Obey The Law of Christ!"

In spite of what some in Christianity now teach, the Apostle Paul knew better than to teach that God's law was discarded. Paul knew what his God said in Malachi 3:6 and also what Jesus taught us in Matthew 7:23.

> **God said: "For I am the LORD [God], I do not change!" Malachi 3:6**
>
> **Jesus said: "Depart from me, you who practice lawlessness." Matthew 7:23**

Meditate on these two Bible teachings and you'll come to the conclusion that the idea the Law has been done away with must not be exactly the whole truth of the matter. God says HE doesn't change and Jesus rejects many Christians who he claims are lawless. IF God's Law were "discarded," why would the Holy Bible have these two teachings?

Jesus' message to the church of Ephesus includes the following compliment.

> **"But this you have [in your favor], that you hate the deeds of the Nicolaitans, which I also hate."**
> **Revelation 2:6**

God told Christ to compliment this church because they hated what the Nicolaitans were doing. In contrast, God told Christ to rebuke the church at Pergamos for having Nicolaitans within their congregation in Revelation 2:14-15. So who were the Nicolaitans?

> **"But I have a few things against you, because you have there those who hold the doctrine of Balaam, who taught Balak to put a stumbling block before the children of Israel, to eat things sacrificed to idols, and to commit sexual immorality. Thus you also have those [in your congregation] who hold the doctrine of the Nicolaitans, which thing I hate. Repent, or else I will come to you quickly and will fight against them with the sword of my mouth. He who has an ear, let him hear what the Spirit says to the churches." Revelation 2:14-17**

The Nicolaitans

Today's Dictionary of The Bible, *1982, Bethany House Publishers*, provides this information on the Nicolaitans.

*"They were seemingly **a class of professing Christians**, who tried to introduce into the church a false freedom or licentiousness, thus abusing Paul's doctrine of grace (compare 2 Peter 2:15, 16, 19), and were probably identical with those who held the doctrine of Balaam (Revelation 2:14)."*

Licentiousness means pursuing your desires very aggressively and selfishly, unchecked by God's morality, especially when it comes to sexual matters (sexually immoral people). Therefore, Nicolaitans claimed that Paul's teachings on grace meant God's laws were discarded and no longer applied to humans.

Nicolaitans claimed Paul taught us the law no longer applied!

A Modern Baptist

"But these, like natural brute beasts made to be caught and destroyed, speak evil of the things they do not understand, and will utterly perish in their own corruption, and will receive the wages of unrighteousness, as those who count it pleasure to carouse in the daytime. They are spots and blemishes, carousing in their own deceptions while they feast with you, having eyes full of adultery and that cannot cease from sin, beguiling unstable souls. They have a heart trained in covetous practices, and are accursed children. They have forsaken the right way and gone astray, following the way of Balaam the son of Beor, who loved the wages of unrighteousness." 2 Peter 2:12-17

In 2 Peter 2:12-22, the Apostle Peter makes it clear that such interpretations of Paul's writing are lies accepted by worldly people who want to feed the desires of their flesh. A complete discussion of this issue is found in "Matters of the Heart" chapter 7. You will find the book online at http://www.bookofedward.org.

One modern Baptist minister on television, who is near the top of this denomination's leadership, has teachings very similar to the Nicolaitans' doctrines and now teaches, "You can't [even] obey the Ten Commandments. That is why God came down and died on the cross for you. HE knew you couldn't obey the commandments." Sound familiar? Maybe you have heard a similar teaching?

When I heard this Baptist televangelist preach this message, the first thought that came to my mind was wondering which of the Ten Commandments he couldn't obey. Was it don't steal? Don't commit adultery? Have no other gods before HIM? Which one?

I <u>Serve</u> The Law Of God

So, from Paul's days to current times, some professing Christians have created doctrines to discard God's laws in favor of a freedom to do anything one wants to do while on this earth. It includes a second chance theology that asserts God's grace will forgive even the most vile and unrepentant sinner from hell and the death of their soul in the lake of fire.

This is not the God of the Holy Bible who makes a distinction between the righteous and unrighteous and calls upon all people to repent of their sins and to obey HIS laws. This is the struggle of all humans: To get out of our flesh (law of sin) and to observe that God gave us a spirit within to serve HIM.

> **Paul said: "So then, with the mind I myself serve the law of God, but with the flesh the law of sin."**
> **Romans 7:25**

You <u>Can</u> Obey God!

God makes a clear distinction between those who are righteous in HIS eyes and those who are ungodly. HIS Word teaches that keeping HIS commandments are not burdensome.

> "For the LORD [God] knows the way of the righteous, but the way of the ungodly shall [lead them to] perish." Psalms 1:6

> "For this is the love of God, that we keep HIS commandments. And [keeping] HIS commandments are not burdensome."
> 1 John 5:3

> Jesus said that it is he or she, "who does the will of my FATHER [God]," that will enter the kingdom of heaven. Matthew 7:21

> Jesus said: "Why do you call me 'Lord, Lord' and do not do the things which I say?"
> Luke 6:46

> Jesus said: "Do not think that I came to destroy [or discard] the Law or the Prophets."
> Matthew 5:17

The truth is that you can obey all of God's Ten Commandments with the sole exception of the fourth commandment **"as the LORD has commanded you."** *This would be a time to read carefully.*

> "Observe the Sabbath day, to keep it holy, <u>as</u> the LORD your God *has commanded you.*"
> Deuteronomy 5:12

The phrase "*as the LORD your God has commanded you*" reflects the fact that God had added many instructions to Jewish law for properly observing the Sabbath day. Ergo, even if you observe the Sabbath on Saturday, which is the correct Sabbath day, you cannot fully obey the fourth commandment unless you comply with all the specific items from God shown in the following verses:

> Exodus 16:23-26
> Exodus 31:15-16
> Exodus 35
> Leviticus 16
> Leviticus 23
> Leviticus 24
> Leviticus 25
> Numbers 15.

Ergo, the fourth commandment is complicated and was designed for Jews, not Christians. And, both Jesus and Paul taught us other aspects about the Sabbath, which need consideration. Obeying the Sabbath Law is not simply a matter of going to church on Saturday or Sunday. People who believe that they are obeying God's fourth commandment by doing so are woefully ignorant of Scripture. For a thorough discussion of God's fourth commandment, see chapter 17 in the *Book of Edward* online at http://www.bookof edward.org.

This does not mean you cannot set aside a day to worship God and to rest your body!

When the Pharisees *saw that Jesus and his disciples* **were not obeying the Sabbath laws**, they complained. In his reply, Jesus said:
> **"The Son of Man [Jesus] is Lord [even] of the Sabbath." Matthew 12:8**

The fact is, when Christ came, the Sabbath laws were changed. Along with these laws, all of the ritual (carnal) laws were cancelled. See Hebrews 9:10 and 2 Corinthians 3:6-18. It would be an insult to God today if anyone went to an altar to sacrifice an animal for the sins of their people. Christ's crucifixion was the final sacrifice for the sins of all people in the world for all time from the beginning to end.

When Paul taught against the law, he was teaching that these ritual laws and especially the ritual of circumcision no longer applied to those "in Christ Jesus." See Galatians 2:15-16 and Galatians 3:15-29. That is why Paul taught us ...

> **"Therefore let no one sit in judgment on you in matters of food and drink, or with regard to a feast day or a New Moon or a Sabbath. Such [things] are only the shadow of things that are to come, and they have only a symbolic value. But the reality (the substance, the solid fact of what is foreshadowed, the body of it) belongs to Christ."**
> **Colossians 2:16-17 (AMP)**

A Sabbath Day Teaching

The issue of the Sabbath is put into a proper perspective by the Gnostic Gospel of Truth, which teaches us the following:

> *"He [Christ] labored even on the Sabbath for the sheep which he found fallen into the pit. He saved the life of that sheep bringing it up from the pit in order that you may understand fully what that Sabbath is, you who possess understanding."*

*"[The Sabbath] is a day in which it is not fitting that salvation be idle, so that you may speak of that heavenly day which has no night and of the sun which does not set because it is perfect. **Say then in your heart that you are this perfect day and that in you the light which does not fail dwells.**"*

IF the Son of God, our Lord Jesus Christ, dwells within your heart, then the Sabbath day dwells within your heart and you *are* this perfect day. It is because *"the light which does not fail"* dwells within you and you are free to worship God anytime day or night. You are not limited to a Saturday, Sunday or any other day. You can worship 24/7 if you want. And, remember Jesus taught ...

"The Sabbath was made for man, and not man for the Sabbath." Mark 2:27

Therefore, always worship God and do not forget to rest your body one day in seven.

Teach The Law

"And these words which I command you today shall be in your heart; you shall teach them diligently to your children, and shall talk of them when you sit in your house, when you walk by the way, when you lie down, and when you rise up. You shall bind them as a sign on your hand, and they shall be as frontlets between your eyes. You shall write them on the doorposts of your house and on your gates." Deuteronomy 6:6-9

> "For the lips of a priest should keep knowledge, and people should seek the law from his mouth; for he is a messenger of the LORD of hosts."
> **Malachi 2:7**
>
> "Preach the Word! Be ready in season and out of season. Convince, rebuke, exhort, with all longsuffering and teaching." **2 Timothy 4:2**

It is clear that God wants us to teach people about HIS laws. It is also clear that some aspects of what could broadly be called "the law" in the Bible have changed. All of the ritual laws provided for in Jewish law no longer apply. This would include tithing and circumcision and animal sacrifices, etc.

In fact, it is the *religious* laws that have been negated. All of the commandments and commands of God have not been changed. And, our call to obey God's commands has not changed.

> **Jesus said:** "I know that HIS command is everlasting life." **John 12:50**
>
> **Jesus said:** "These things I command you, that you love one another." **John 15:17**
>
> "[Jesus] became the author of eternal salvation <u>to all who</u> **obey** [God]." **Hebrews 5:9**

Summation Of The Law

If all of this sounds a little confusing at times, it can be. However, Jesus *did* simplify the essence of the law in the Gospel of Matthew.

> **Jesus said: " 'You shall love the LORD your God with all your heart, with all your soul, and with all your mind.' This is the first and great commandment. And the second is like it: 'You shall love your neighbor as yourself.' On these two commandments hang all the Law and the Prophets." Matthew 22:37-39**

Jesus teaches us that obeying the Law is as simple as obeying two commandments. If we do this, our spirit will express God's love into the world and will lead us home to our eternal life in Heaven. It is extremely hard to willfully sin if we are faithful to observe the above two commandments from God. This doesn't make us perfect as the Bible teaches, "we are made perfect before God through Christ Jesus our Lord." [Colossians 1:28, John 17:23] We will still have unknown and unintentional sins in our life. And, we will get into the midst of sin without realizing how we got there. When this happens, it is time for further repentance with God. We also need to step out of sin when we find ourselves involved. In short, we need to do the right thing in terms of what God would have us do.

Summation Of Sin

The issue of what is called sin can also be confusing. What one church allows, another might call sin. However, God has a simple standard for sin in the Bible that applies to every individual and circumstance no matter what his or her education happens to be. This even includes those with a very limited knowledge of God and HIS human begotten Son Jesus.

> **"Therefore, to him who knows to do good and does not do it, to him it is sin." James 4:17**

> "So any person who knows what is right to do but does not do it, to him it is sin."
> **James 4:17 AMP**

Everyone knows the right thing to do for any given situation they find themselves in and regardless of their education. Why is this?

God's Internal Program

How is it that we know the right thing to do in any given situation or circumstance, regardless of our education or background? God HIMSELF has programmed part of our minds and hearts!

> God says: "I will put MY law in their minds and write it on their hearts; and I will be their God, and they shall be MY people. No more shall every man teach his neighbor, and every man his brother, saying 'Know the LORD,' for they shall all know ME." Jeremiah 31:33-34

> "[God] has put eternity in [our] hearts, except that [none of us] can find out the work that God does from the beginning to end."
> **Ecclesiastes 3:11**

Like an internal computer program, every human heart and mind knows what is right. If we know what is right, why is it that many continue to do wrong and thereby sin? The trouble lies in the fact that most people will not take the time to "listen" to the spirit that God has put inside us. God's Spirit speaks to our spirit in a soft and quiet voice. In order to communicate with HIM, we need to slow down, quiet the internal noise of our mind, and quiet the external background noise around us that inhibits our spiritual hearing.

> "Be still, and know that I am God; I will be exalted among the nations, I will be exalted in the earth!" Psalms 46:10

Once we escape the physical limitations that surround our minds and we start to focus on the spiritual realm, we can begin to hear God very clearly. We have, as the old saying goes, "tuned in" to God. At that point we have become spiritually alive and born again unto God. Then, doing what's right is easy.

It's Really About Righteousness

Many preach there is no salvation without going through Jesus Christ. However, this is not what Jesus taught us about salvation. He taught that it was all about righteousness. He called everyone to repent and stated clearly that if they didn't, they would not enter the kingdom of heaven. Jesus' teachings are the same as those found in the Old Testament given to us by other prophets of God.

> "I know that whatever God does, it shall be forever. Nothing can be added to it, and nothing taken from it. God does it, that men should fear before HIM." Ecclesiastes 3:14

> "Then Peter opened his mouth and said: 'In truth I perceive that God shows no partiality. But in every nation *whoever* fears HIM and works righteousness is accepted by HIM.' "
> Acts 10:34-35

What Peter is saying is simple. The salvation Christ taught us in the New Testament is the same salvation as taught in Ezekiel 18 and in many other parts of the Old Testament. The idea that anyone who does not know Christ is destined for hell is a false doctrine found in the Church at large. Christ always pointed us back to his FATHER, whom he called our God.

Christ's teachings taught us to repent and return to God. We do that by acknowledging God exists and that He expects us to live a righteous life to Him while on this earth.

Ergo, everyone who lives unto righteousness is acceptable to God no matter what country they live in, what ethnicity they are, and no matter what religion they claim. However, God will not accept idol worshippers. If your religion worships any idols, bows down to them or offers sacrifices, you do not know God. Having said this, Christ is God's gift to us. Why?

Those who are baptized in the name of Jesus will receive God's Holy Spirit. Jesus and God, the Father, will then come and live within them guiding their spirits back to their own heavenly mansion. While all of mankind is free to search for God on their own, they are also free to acknowledge Jesus as God's gift to us that helps our spiritual search for truth. Jesus is *the* Teacher and when we learn from him and follow his teachings, we get on a fast track to fellowship with our God.

Thus, we can choose to be taught by Jesus, the Christ, who was sent by God Himself to make it spiritually easier on us to get home. Doing so results in getting God's Holy Spirit abundantly.

Without Jesus Christ in our lives, it is like wandering through a big city without a map or any idea of where we are going and what we are searching for. With Christ, spiritual clarity comes to our mind and all we have to do is follow the teachings of Christ.

Salvation and eternal life follows a spiritual choice to repent and live unto righteousness.

> **"For the eyes of the Lord are on the righteous, and His ears are open to their prayers; but the face of the Lord is against those who do evil."**
> **1 Peter 3:12**

> **"[You, who through Jesus] believe in [the] God, who raised [Jesus] from the dead and gave him glory, *so that your faith and hope are in God.*"**
> **1 Peter 1:21**

Jesus' purpose is well expressed by Peter. It was so that "your faith and hope would be in God." To put this in another way, Jesus did not come so you could worship him. Jesus came to bring you back to his God.

> **"[God is] not willing that any should perish but that all [people] should come to repentance [and eternal life]." 2 Peter 3:9**

Locked Out Of Heaven

Finally on the Law, we see in Romans 1:18, 1 Corinthians 6:9-10 and in Revelation 22:15 that the following 15 types of people are excluded from heaven. It is obvious God's laws are still relevant!

1. Unrighteous
2. Ungodly
3. Fornicators
4. Adulterers
5. Homosexuals
6. Sodomites
7. Thieves
8. Drunkards
9. Revilers
10. Sexually immoral
11. Sorcerers
12. Murderers
13. Idolaters
14. Lovers of lies
15. Practitioners of lies

Christ's Higher Standard

You have learned:

1. God's laws have not been discarded.

2. Jewish laws have been discarded.

3. Christ changed the Sabbath laws and yet you can still worship God and take time out to rest your body, as the Sabbath day commandment basically asks us to do.

4. Salvation is really about repentance and righteousness. Those *locked out of heaven* are unrighteous and lawless in God's eyes.

Before focusing on the **Law of Christ**, you needed to understand the role of repentance and righteousness in obtaining salvation and eternal life. God gave a higher righteousness standard to Christ so that our sensitivity to sin would be increased. Not only do evil deeds get us in trouble, but the unrighteous thoughts that lead us to commit evil deeds also get us into trouble.

Therefore, the *Law of Christ* is God's call to a higher righteousness standard. HE calls us to become more sensitive towards sin in our life. Those who walk closely with God are very sensitive to the issue of sin and do not want even an *appearance* of sin to occur. In using a basic legal analogy, the *Law of Christ* calls on us to follow the Spirit of God's laws and not just the letter of HIS laws.

Ergo, we don't look for legal loopholes within God's written word, as modern day lawyers would do with any of man's written laws.

Consider the issue of the tattoo as a simple illustration of what I am talking about. It is written ...

> **"You shall not make any cuttings in your flesh for the dead, nor tattoo any marks on you; [for] I am the LORD [your God]." Leviticus 19:28**

We do not get any reasons or explanations for God's instructions to not tattoo our body. This is very popular in today's culture, but it begs the question: Exactly how close is your walk with God? Is it close enough to obey HIS commands even when HE gives you no reason for doing so? When you can answer yes to this question, you are talking with God and walking in faith. You have begun your spiritual adventure with God.

You can study the *Law of Christ* in the three chapters of Matthew 5-7. I will give you a few illustrations below and, now that you know the *Law of Christ* represents a call from God to an increased righteousness standard, you can understand what Christ is teaching and why God gave him these instructions.

> **"You have heard that it was said to those of old, 'You shall not murder,' and whosoever murders will be in danger of the judgment. But I say to you that whosoever is angry with his brother without a cause shall be in danger of the [sin of murder] judgment." Matthew 5:21-22**

In this illustration, Christ teaches us to watch our thoughts of anger without cause against our brother. Unrighteous mental thoughts with anger can lead to murder. Christ then teaches us to reconcile ourselves with our brothers before bringing a gift to God's altar. In other words, don't come to God when "*your brother has something against you!*" Note: This is an increase in righteousness standards!

> **"You have heard that it was said to those of old, 'You shall not commit adultery,' but I say to you that whoever looks at a woman to lust for her has already committed adultery with her in his heart." Matthew 5:27-28**

Christ isn't talking about a man looking at a woman in an admiring way. Christ is talking about a man whose "*heart*" is "*lusting*" for a woman. It means the man has plans for sex with the woman and it doesn't involve love and marriage, but unrighteous fornication. Note: This is also an increase in righteousness standards.

Chapter 19 in the *Book of Edward* has a detailed discussion on our human sexuality. You will find it at http://www.bookofedward.org.

> **"You have heard that it was said, 'An eye for an eye and a tooth for a tooth,' but I tell you not to resist an evil person. But whoever slaps you on your right cheek, turn the other to him also."**
> **Matthew 5:38-39**

Christ **IS NOT** teaching you to roll over and allow evil to have its way in your life. Christ is teaching you to show more than just raw human emotions to the people of *this* world. After all, you are supposed to have God's Spirit inside you. If so, then you will be able to respond with a spiritual response and not just as an ordinary human would respond. Why? It is because God's Spirit has taken you beyond the physical limits of our earthly existence and has shown you that you have a heavenly mansion waiting for you. Let *your response* show your adversary God's love, God's ways and the fact that you belong to HIM! Note: This is another increase in God's righteousness standards.

> "You have heard that it was said, 'You shall love your neighbor and hate your enemy,' but I say to you, love your enemies, bless those who curse you, and pray for those who spitefully use you and persecute you." Matthew 5:43-44

Again, Christ **IS NOT** teaching you to let an enemy rule over your life. Christ is teaching you a higher righteousness standard. He is teaching you to show your enemies God's love and adds: "For if you [only] love those who love you, what reward have you?" In fact, isn't it true that all humans bless those they love and pray for those they love? What makes a child of God different than those in the massive crowd headed towards Hell? It is God's Spirit in us!

Show People The Love Of God That Is Inside Of You!

The *Law of Christ* is a higher standard of righteousness and love that we have been given by God through Christ. When we obey the *Law of Christ* like Paul did, we subscribe to the Spirit of God's Laws and not just the letter of God's Laws. In the process, we walk closer with God and we are much more sensitive to any act of sin that might separate us from God's Spirit.

> "And you know that [Christ] was manifested to take away our sins, and in [Christ] there is no sin. Whoever abides in [Christ] does not sin. Whoever sins has neither seen [Christ] nor known [Christ]. Little children, let no one deceive you. He who practices righteousness is righteous, just as [Christ] is righteous. He who sins is of the devil." 1 John 3:5-8

The Seven Spirits

> **Orthodox Christianity teaches God is a triune God expressed by three entities. God the FATHER + God the Holy Spirit + God the Son = 3. As a result, many Christians now worship Jesus as God and commit idolatry. However, the Bible teaches that there are seven Spirits of God and identifies all of them. I.E. We read in Revelation 1:4, "Grace to you and peace from HIM [God] who is and who was and who is to come, and from the SEVEN SPIRITS who are before HIS [God's] throne, and [also] from Jesus Christ." The math is 1+7+1=9, not 3!**
>
> **Apostle Edward**

Bible Reference: Revelation 1:4

The Seven Spirits Contents

	Page
The Seven Spirits	121
The Seven Spirits Graphic	123
Who Is And Who Was And Who Is To Come	124-125
Six Attributes of God	125
Six Attributes of Jesus	126
Orthodox Math Error	126
God Gave Jesus All Seven Spirits	127
Seven Spirits Sent Into All The Earth	127-128
Church Tradition Negates God's Holy Word	128
God Is Not A Man	129-131
The Seven Spirits Identified	131-132
Seven Spirits Summary Table	133-134
Return To M<small>E</small>	134-137
Seven Spirits of God Personal Survey Checklist	138

The Seven Spirits Graphic

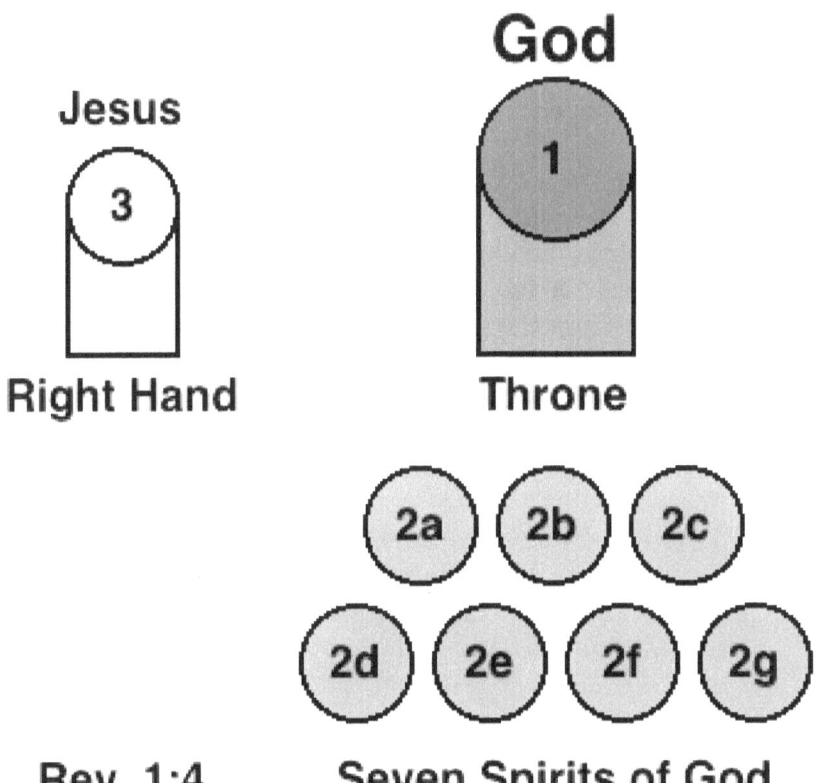

God + Seven Spirits + Jesus = 9

[God] "Who Is And Who Was And Who Is To Come"

[Apostle] John,

TO the seven churches which are in Asia:

"Grace to you and peace from HIM [God] who is and who was and who is to come, *and* from the seven Spirits who are before HIS throne, *and* from Jesus Christ, the faithful witness, the firstborn from the dead, and the ruler over the kings of the earth [who sits at the right hand of God Almighty]." Revelation 1:4-5

PRAISE BE UNTO [Jesus]:

"Who loved us and washed us from our sins in his own blood, and has made us kings and priests to his God and FATHER, to him [then] be glory and dominion forever and ever. Amen."
                                          Revelation 1:5-6

Observe that God is on the throne and HE is described or characterized as [HE] "who is and who was and who is to come."

In Revelation 1:8, the identity of the ALPHA and OMEGA is *also* characterized as [HE] "who is and who was and who is to come." Some Bibles imply that Jesus is the ALPHA and OMEGA, but this is *only* a reference to God ALMIGHTY. *The New American Standard Bible [NASB] clarifies the verse as follows:*

" 'I am the ALPHA and the OMEGA,' says the LORD God, who is and who was and who is to come, the ALMIGHTY." Revelation 1:8 (NASB)

"And when I [John] saw [Jesus], I fell at his feet. But he laid his right hand on me, saying to me, 'Do not be afraid; I am the first and the last, I am he who lives, *and was dead*, and behold, I am [now] alive forevermore. And, I have the keys of Hades and of Death.' " Revelation 1:17-18

Six Attributes Of God

1	[HIM] who is and who was and who is to come
2	Sits on throne
3	Seven Spirits before HIS throne
4	Jesus sits by HIS right hand
5	God ALMIGHTY
6	ALPHA and OMEGA

In Revelation, we see the above attributes of God identified. Note that SEVEN SPIRITS are before God's throne and that they belong to HIM. We also see some attributes that are identified as belonging to Jesus. Note these *are* distinctions between God and Jesus!

Six Attributes Of Jesus

1	Faithful Witness
2	Firstborn of the dead
3	Ruler over kings of earth
4	Washed us with his blood
5	Makes us kings & priests to God
6	His God is the FATHER on throne

Jesus gives Apostle John the messages for the seven churches. Remember that Jesus has taught us that he only speaks and does what God tells him to say and do. Therefore, these are God's messages and warnings for the seven churches delivered through Jesus and the human hand of John.

Orthodox Math Error

So, we see something different emerging from the word of God. There are actually SEVEN SPIRITS and not just one. The Orthodox Christian doctrine called the trinity, which created a triune God, ignores six of the seven or 85.7% of God's Spirits.

You might surmise that if you ignored 85.7% of any given subject, that you are for the most part completely ignorant of the subject. For example, would a final grade of 14.3% on any type of exam satisfy you? Is it any different with the *seven* Spirits of God?

Can we really claim to know God when we are ignorant of HIS *seven* Spirits? If you believe in the trinity doctrine, the math does not add up now when it comes to the Spirits of God. Jesus *plus* the FATHER [God] *plus* HIS *seven* Spirits is nine, not three as when *only* the Holy Spirit is considered and counted.

God Gave Jesus All Seven Spirits

And to the angel of the church in Sardis write, "These things says he [Jesus] who *has* [all of] the *seven* Spirits of God and the seven stars: 'I know your works, that you have a name that you are alive, but you are dead.' " Revelation 3:1

"And from the throne proceeded lightnings, thunderings, and voices. Seven lamps of fires were burning before the throne [of God], which are the *seven* Spirits of God." Revelation 4:5

"And I looked, and behold, in the midst of the throne and of the four living creatures, and in the midst of the elders, stood a Lamb [Jesus] as though it had been slain, having seven horns and seven eyes, which are the *seven* Spirits of God <u>sent out into all the earth</u>." Revelation 5:6

Seven Spirits Sent Into All The Earth

God sent all seven of HIS Spirits into all the earth. How many can you name? For most Christians, the answer would be one. The Holy Spirit or Spirit of Truth taught as part of the triune God doctrine of the Church.

The Church through its doctrine of the trinity has created a God that is not the God that Jesus knew and worshipped. The trinity doctrine raises some important questions about God.

A) Exactly which God did Jesus say we were *to worship and serve* in Matthew 4:10?

B) Exactly which God did Jesus say *he was returning to* in John 20:17?

C) Exactly which God did Jesus say was *the only true God* in John 17:3?

D) Exactly which God did Jesus say *we were to listen to* in John 8:47?

It wasn't Jesus who created the idea that he was "God the Son." It was the Catholic Church at the First Council of Nicea in 325 AD. The apostles worshipped the same God that Jesus worshipped. It was the God of the Jews. I've heard some Christians gasp for air exclaiming: "You mean we are supposed to worship the God of the Jews?" The answer is yes. And, the fact that even one Christian can make such an exclamation shows that the Church has created a different God than the one worshipped by Jesus and his disciples.

Church Tradition Negates God's Holy Word

The scribes and Pharisees asked Jesus why his disciples [negated the effect of or] transgressed the tradition of the elders. Jesus answered and said to them,

> **"Why do you [scribes and Pharisees] also transgress [negate] the commandment of God because of your tradition?" Matthew 15:3**

Jesus would now ask the Church, "Why do you transgress the commandment of God to have no other gods before HIM because of your trinity tradition?" Apostle Edward

Yes, the trinity doctrine transgresses God's commandment to have no other gods before HIM. This commandment includes HIS only begotten human Son Jesus Christ. There are now Christians who worship Jesus, a human *man* according to the Bible, as their God. A complete discussion of the trinity doctrine is in my book *Trinity Dogma*. You can find it online at http://www.trinitydogma.com.

God Is Not A Man

> "God is not a man that HE should lie, nor a son of man, that HE should repent. Has HE said, and will HE not do it? Or has HE spoken, and will HE not make it good?" Numbers 23:19

Orthodox theologies and doctrines explain away or argue around simple verses like this one by claiming Jesus was simultaneously both 100% man and 100% God. Ergo, Jesus was even able to worship himself?

All such teachings are nonsense and God's Word stands firmly as it is written. It does not need to be interpreted through a man-made trinity doctrine that was *created* by the Church in 325 AD.

Some may want to explain away these *seven* Spirits. However, I must warn them. Those who speak against God's *seven* Spirits may be guilty of blaspheming God's Holy Spirit. Ergo, dismiss God's seven Spirits at your own risk of committing the one sin that Jesus taught us was unforgivable by God. The Holy Spirit is also called the Spirit of Truth. Therefore, anyone who simply dismisses God's seven Spirits as irrelevant is engaged in lies. Caution is due here.

> **"Hear, O Israel [all of God's people]: The LORD our God, the LORD is ONE. You shall love the LORD your God with all your heart, with all your soul, and with all your might."**
> **Deuteronomy 6:4-5**

When Moses proclaimed to God's people that the LORD God was ONE, he was trying to educate them. The Egyptians had multiple gods. No doubt, Moses wanted to make it very clear, there was just *one* true God. This isn't all that complicated.

The word "one" means exactly "one". There is no place in the Bible where you will find any "three" or "trinity" proclamation. So, exactly who was the God that Moses talked to? Wasn't it the same God Jesus prayed to and worshipped? And, isn't it clear that God did not manifest HIMSELF to Moses via three different entities? The trinity doctrine makes Moses appear as a liar. Did Moses lie to us?

So, if there are actually *seven* Spirits of God and the Bible teaches that the LORD God is ONE, how do we explain the trinity doctrine?

We see from historical documents attributed to Ignatius, the third bishop of Antioch, that he taught the trinity doctrine in the latter part of the first century and maybe as early as 80 or 90 A.D. In *The Epistle of Ignatius to the Ephesians*, [chapter 4, v13] we read: "God himself appearing in the form of a man."

As the early Church was forming, it created the trinity doctrine and then began to teach it as orthodoxy and absolute biblical truth.

I attribute this deception to Satan with the full intent to lead man astray and away from God. Much of the Bible, as we know it, was not available in the early years. Today, with modern Bible software, there is no excuse for perpetuating the satanic and evil doctrine of the trinity upon the people.

The trinity doctrine is satanic and evil because it leads people away from the one true God and has many now worshipping another god in place of HIM. What an incredible insult the trinity is to our God who sacrificed HIS only begotten human Son Jesus.

Those who claim Christ was anything more than a human in the flesh reflect the spirit of the Antichrist. The Apostle John writes:

> **"And every spirit that does not confess that Jesus Christ has come in the flesh is not of God. And this is the spirit of the Antichrist, which you have heard was coming, and is now already in the world." 1 John 4:3**

If you believe that Jesus was not all human [flesh], you have the spirit of the Antichrist. I didn't teach it; the Apostle John taught it. However, I will teach you this: The trinity doctrine is the deceptive work of Satan designed particularly for these End Times.

The Seven Spirits Identified

Now that you know that there are *seven* Spirits of God sent into all the earth and that Jesus had them all at his disposal, exactly who are these Spirits? You will find God's *seven* Spirits fully identified in the Bible at the following Scripture references. Check it out.

> **"The Spirit of the LORD [God], (sent into all the earth) shall rest upon him [Jesus],
> The Spirit of wisdom and understanding,
> The Spirit of counsel and might,
> The Spirit of knowledge and of the fear of the LORD [God]." Isaiah 11:2**

> "And I will pour on the house of David and on the inhabitants of Jerusalem the Spirit of grace and supplication; then they will look on me whom they pierced. Yes, they will mourn for him as one mourns for his only son, and grieve for him as one grieves for a firstborn."
> **Zechariah 12:10**

> "The Spirit of truth, whom the world cannot receive, because it neither sees [GOD] nor knows [GOD]; but you know [GOD], for HE dwells with you and will be in you." **John 14:17**

The *Contemporary English Version*, *New Living Translation* and other bibles refer to the Spirit of Truth as the Holy Spirit. This is not the same Spirit as the Spirit of Holiness.

> "And declared to be the Son of God with power according to the Spirit of holiness, by the resurrection from the dead." **Romans 1:4**

> "If you are reproached for the name of Christ, blessed are you, for the Spirit of glory and of God rests upon you. On their part he is blasphemed, but on your part he is glorified."
> **1 Peter 4:14**

Like the thousands of trinity rationalizations found online, there are literally thousands of ways these Scriptures are dismissed. One way claims that these are seven manifestations of the Holy Spirit. Really? Is that what Jesus, who was given all SEVEN SPIRITS by God would tell you? People seek to dismiss God's seven Spirits, because it is inconsistent with the trinity doctrine. Ergo, Scripture that speaks directly against the trinity is usually rationalized away.

Seven Spirits Summary Table

Specific Identities of God's Seven Spirits	Bible Reference
Spirit of Wisdom and Understanding	Isaiah 11:2
Spirit of Counsel and Might	Isaiah 11:2
Spirit of Knowledge and Fear of the LORD	Isaiah 11:2
Spirit of Grace and Supplication	Zechariah 12:10
Spirit of Truth	John 14:17
Spirit of Holiness	Romans 1:4
Spirit of Glory	1 Peter 4:14

There is a lot more to God's Spirits that could be studied. Note that the Scripture references point directly to Jesus Christ. These are the *seven* Spirits that God gave Christ. They are *also* the seven Spirits that God sent into all the earth.

How many Spirits of God have been given to you? It is my prayer that more than one has, because I do not believe you are saved unless you at least have the Spirit of the Fear of the LORD and the Spirit of Truth. Certain Scriptures indicate this; some of them have been discussed in the other chapters and more information is online in the Book of Edward at http://www.bookofedward.org. Also, see http://www.trinitydogma.com for further information on the trinity.

Isn't it curious that the Spirit of truth is sent back to those who begin a new life in Christ Jesus? It is because God's manifested power in our new life begins with His truth. When you can believe HIM instead of the Church! Where does God's Word fit into your own life? Will you die for HIM like Jesus did? How strong is your conviction to know the truth and nothing but the truth?

Can we honestly say we know God if we do not know HIS seven Spirits? And, if we do know HIS seven Spirits, can we still believe in a man made Church doctrine called the trinity? A doctrine that denies the God found in the Bible and substitutes a man made and Church created, triune pagan god?

Pagan god? Harsh sounding, yes, I know. But isn't that exactly what any man made triune god is? The Orthodox triune god is *not* the God of Moses and *not* the God of Jesus! And, it is *not* the God of Abraham! God lamented to Moses the following:

> **"Oh, that they [MY people] had such a heart in them that they would fear ME and always keep all MY commandments, that it [everything] might be well with them and with their children forever!" Deuteronomy 5:29**

Return To ME

> **"And the LORD commanded us to observe all these statutes, to fear the LORD our God, for our good always, that HE might preserve us alive, as it is this day. Then it will be righteousness for us, if we are careful to observe all these commandments before the LORD our God, as HE has commanded us." Deuteronomy 6:24-25**

There is nothing that God has asked us to do that is not for our own good. When we learn to fear God, we also learn to obey HIM. And we find out that God only wants the best for our lives and the lives of our children. Still, God's people have a history of leaving God behind and ignoring HIM. And yet, God has continually sought fellowship with man.

At the heart of Jesus' teachings is the firm instruction to return to God ALMIGHTY.

This means that our God is a personal God that wants to be involved in our lives and not an impersonal God that could care less about us. Listen carefully to a very personal dialog as Jesus talks with his [and our] God.

> "FATHER, the hour has come. Glorify YOUR Son that YOUR Son may also glorify YOU, as YOU have given him authority over all flesh, that he should give eternal life to as many as YOU have given him. And this is eternal life, that they may know YOU, the only true God, and Jesus Christ whom YOU have sent." John 17:1-3

Jesus isn't talking to himself or to 1/3rd of a fictitious triune god. Jesus is talking to God HIMSELF, the FATHER, which is "the only true God!"

Jesus Said: "YOU, [Are] The *Only* True God!"

> "Then Jesus cried out and said, 'He who [truly] believes in me, believes not in me but [actually believes] in HIM who sent me.' " John 12:44

You cannot claim to have received the gift of salvation unless you know the God that Jesus knew. His purpose was to help you return to God: to give you an understanding of HIM so that you would have eternal life. Jesus did not come to us with God's Word so he could personally supplant his God in our hearts. You don't know Jesus if you do not know YAHWEH, the God that Jesus served.

> **"And we know that the Son of God has come and has given us an understanding that we know [God] who is true; and we are in [God] who is true, in HIS Son Jesus Christ. [Christ's God] is the [only] true God and [the only] eternal life." 1 John 5:20**

"You shall have <u>no</u> other gods before ME!" Deuteronomy 5:7

The lamentation of God that things would go well for us if we only feared HIM and obeyed HIS commands is clear. Yet, God also lamented, "if *only* we would return to HIM." When all else is said, it was God's clear purpose that HIS Son would help us "return to HIM" by making HIS reality and the reality of an eternal life after this earthly existence clearer to us. *Even today, God wants a personal relationship with you and asks that you return to HIM.* Will you? Will you accept the God that Jesus reintroduced us to? The God who has *seven* Spirits?

"Return to ME, for I have redeemed you!" Isaiah 44:22

> **"If you [MY people] will return, O Israel," says the LORD, return to ME; And if you will put away your abominations out of MY sight, then you shall not be moved. And you will swear, 'The LORD [God] lives.' " Jeremiah 4:1**

> "Then I will give them a heart to know ME, that I am the LORD; and they shall be MY people, and I will be their God, for they shall return to ME with their whole heart." Jeremiah 24:7

> "Return to the LORD your God, for HE is gracious and merciful." Joel 2:12

> "And it shall come to pass that whoever calls on the name of the LORD [YAHWEH] shall be saved." Joel 2:32

The *New Jerusalem Bible* expresses the above verse as follows. The verses are numbered slightly different in the NJB.

> "All who call on the name of YAHWEH will be saved." Joel 3:5 (NJB)

****

God has *Seven* Spirits before HIS throne!

****

Think About It!

Seven Spirits of God
Personal Survey Checklist

✔	#	God's Seven Spirits
	1	Spirit of Wisdom and Understanding
	2	Spirit of Counsel and Might
	3	Spirit of Knowledge and Fear of the LORD
	4	Spirit of Grace and Supplication
	5	Spirit of Truth
	6	Spirit of Holiness
	7	Spirit of Glory

Instructions: The descriptions of God's Spirits are self-evident as to their intended purposes. Place a checkmark next to each Spirit you believe that God has given you to support you during this earthly life. I pray God has given you #3 and #5 at a minimum. Without the fear of God, there is little chance of true obedience to HIS Word. Without the Spirit of Truth, there is no baptism of the Spirit, which is the result of truly accepting Christ Jesus into our hearts. Ergo, we must be obedient to God's Word and lovers of HIS truth. And, without having received these two Spirits I do not believe that one is truly saved. It is yet another aspect of salvation not talked about by the Church. *Apostle Edward*

The Tithe Lie

> "[Jesus] sent his disciples to preach the kingdom of God and to heal the sick. And he said to them, 'Take nothing for the journey, neither staffs nor bag nor bread nor money; and do not have two tunics apiece.' " AND, when Jesus sent out seventy more, he told them: "Go your way, behold, I send you out as lambs among wolves. Carry neither money bag, sack, nor sandals." AND "Jesus said to them, 'When I sent you without money bag, sack, and sandals, did you lack anything?' So they said, 'Nothing!' "
>
> Apostle Edward

Bible References: Luke 9:2-3; Luke 10:3-4; Luke 22:35

The Tithe Lie Contents

	Page
Cover – Jesus' Words	141
Basis Of Tithe Lie	143
Discussion	143-146
Apostle's Warning	146
The Tithe Law	147-148
God's Tithe Instructions	148-152
Tithe Law Graphic Summary	149
Man's Tithe Instructions	152-153
Today's Tithe Essence	153-154
What Jesus Taught	154-157
Seven Giving Principles	158-159
Giving Directly To God	159

Basis Of Tithe Lie

> "Will a man rob God?
> Yet you have robbed ME!
> But you say,
> 'In what way have we robbed YOU?'
> In tithes and offerings.
>
> You are cursed with a curse,
> For you have robbed ME,
> Even this whole nation.
> Bring all the tithes into the storehouse,
> That there may be food in MY house,
>
> And prove ME now in this,"
> Says the LORD of hosts,
> "If I will not open for you the windows
>   of heaven
> And pour out for you such blessing
> That there will not be *room* enough *to receive it.*"
>   **Malachi 3:8-10**

This Scripture in Malachi is the basis of the tithe lie. It is a very powerful Scripture. Who among us wants to rob God? The experienced tithe preacher plays on our emotions to teach that we rob God in two distinct ways using this Scripture. First, we fail to tithe [give the Church 10% of our gross income], and second, we fail to give offerings [in *addition* to the tithe]. I have heard many tithe teachings that use Malachi, but this is not the only Scripture abused.

I believed in tithing for a season. Anyone with a heart that wants to get close to God would be horrified to think they might be robbing HIM. However, if they know God's Word, they can reject the tithe lie as a false teaching. They may also want to find a new teacher.

At best, a tithe teacher is ignorant of God's Word. If they are not ignorant, then they are liars, because they know better than to add or subtract from God's Word.

I can hear someone's voice saying: "Apostle Edward, aren't you being harsh calling tithe teachers either ignorant of God's Word or liars?" No, I don't think I am. I believe that those two characterizations fully explain tithe teachers, regardless of their pedigrees or popularity or size of their ministry. This will become fully apparent to you by the end of this chapter. For now, consider some Scripture:

> **"Some, having strayed, have turned aside to idle talk, desiring to be teachers of the law, understanding neither what they say nor the things they affirm." 1 Timothy 1:7-8**
>
> **Jesus said [to some teachers]: "You are mistaken, not knowing the Scriptures nor the power of God." Matthew 22:29**
>
> **"My brethren, let not many of you become teachers, knowing that we shall receive a stricter judgment." James 3:1**
>
> **"So any person who knows what is right to do but does not do it, to him it is sin."**
> **James 4:17 (AMP)**
>
> **"For the time will come when they will not endure sound doctrine, but according to their own desires, because they have itching ears, they will heap up for themselves teachers; and they will turn their ears away from the truth, and be turned aside to fables." 2 Timothy 4:3-4**

FACT: False and ignorant teachers have existed from time immemorial, but in these End-Times, it is ever more prevalent today. Scripture must fully support Bible doctrines!

The above Scriptures make it clear that God will hold teachers to a higher standard. This higher standard is reflected in James 4:17. Every teacher of God's Word should *know* not to add or subtract from HIS words.

> **"Whoever loves and practices a lie [is not allowed into the kingdom of heaven]."**
> **Revelation 22:15**

This Scripture refers to a lover of lies, not a person who tells a white lie here or there. A complete discussion of the issue of lying can be found in the *Book Of Edward, Volume I,* starting at page 83.

FACT: The tithe preacher lies about God's Word in Malachi 3 to raise money for their ministry and for their own personal gain.

> **"Whatever I [God] command you [to do], be careful to observe it; you shall not add to it nor take away from it." Deuteronomy 12:32**
>
> **"Every word of God is pure; HE is a shield to those who put their trust in HIM. Do not add to HIS words, lest HE rebuke you, and you be found a liar." Psalms 30:5-6**
>
> **"If anyone adds to these things, God will add to him the plagues that are written in this book; and if anyone takes away from the words of the book of this prophecy, God shall take away his part from the Book of Life, from the holy city, and from the things which are written in this book." Revelation 22:18-19**

"God is not a man, that HE should lie, Nor a son of man, that HE should repent. Has HE said, and will HE not do it? Or has HE spoken, and will HE not make it good?" Numbers 23:19

FACT: God has made it clear we are not to add or subtract from HIS Word. And that if we do, there are serious consequences.

Apostle's Warning

God has several issues with tithe teachers. If you teach tithing, consider this as a warning from God to stop perverting HIS Holy Word for your own financial gain. You cannot serve God and money. Choose who your true master is! Edward

By teaching tithing, you ...

- **ADD to and SUBTRACT from God's Holy Word.**

- **PERVERT God's Word for ministry and personal gain.**

- **IDENTIFY yourself as a lover and practitioner of lies.**

- **WILL BE ACCOUNTABLE to God's higher teacher standard.**

And Jesus said: "[Woe] to whoever causes one of these [another] ... to sin!" Matthew 18:6-7

The Tithe Law

Deuteronomy 14:22-29

[22] "You shall truly tithe all the increase of your grain that the field produces year by year.

[23] And you shall eat before the LORD your God, in the place where HE chooses to make HIS name abide, the tithe of your grain and your new wine and your oil, of the firstborn of your herds and your flocks, *that you may learn to fear the LORD your God always.*

[24] But if the journey is too long for you, so that you are not able to carry the tithe, or if the place where the LORD your God chooses to put HIS name is too far from you, when the LORD your God has blessed you, [25] then you shall exchange it for money, take the money in your hand, and go to the place which the LORD your God chooses. [26] And you shall spend that money for whatever your heart desires ...

[For whatever your heart desires]: for oxen or sheep, for wine or similar drink, for whatever your heart desires; you shall eat there before the LORD your God, and you shall rejoice, you and your household. [27] You shall not forsake the Levite who is within your gates, for he has no part nor inheritance with you."

[28] "At the end of every third year you shall bring out the tithe of your produce of that year and store it up within your gates."

[29] And the Levite, because he has no portion nor inheritance with you, and the stranger and the fatherless and the widow who are within your gates, may come and eat and be satisfied, that the LORD your God may bless you in all the work of your hand which you do."
Deuteronomy 14:22-29

God's Tithe Instructions

There are TWO purposes cited by God in the "Tithe Law" HE gave the Hebrews.

1. So you could **learn** to fear the LORD your God always. [v23]

2. So **food** would be available for the Levite, the stranger, the fatherless, and the widows within your *gates* [those close to you or within your community, neighborhood]. [v28-29]

There are THREE yearly instructions.

1. **Year 1** – Consume your tithe before the LORD. Don't forget to bring the Levites to the worship celebration.

2. **Year 2** – Same as year one.

3. **Year 3** – Bring your tithe [food] to a storehouse so other people could eat.

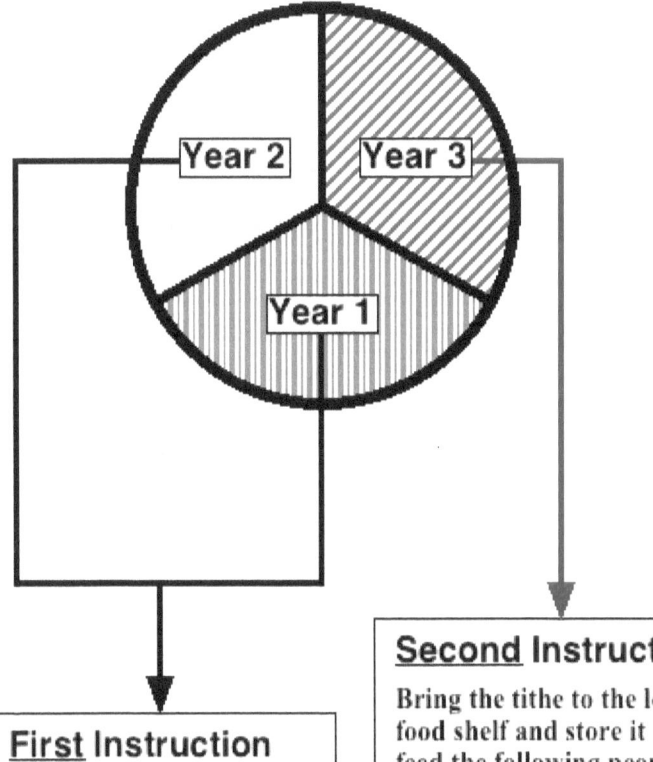

Three Year Tithe Law Instructions

First Instruction

Household consumes tithe in a celebration to teach the fear of the LORD our God. Don't forget to bring the minister with you.
[Deuteronomy 14:22-27]

Second Instruction

Bring the tithe to the local food shelf and store it up to feed the following people:
a) Minister
b) Stranger
c) Temporary Resident
d) Fatherless
e) Widow
[Deuteronomy 14:27-28]

There are <u>FIVE</u> things God wanted tithed.

1. Tithe the grain harvest. [v22-23]
2. Tithe the new wine.
3. Tithe the new oil.
4. Tithe the firstborn of your herds.
5. Tithe the firstborn of your flocks.

God said to tithe against HIS INCREASE.

God's increase in the yield applies. [Gross yield less input or costs = actual increase.] For example, if you planted 10 bushels of corn and only harvested 10 bushels of corn, there was no increase. If you harvested 20 bushels, your increase was 10, and you tithed 1 bushel of corn. God only expected you to tithe on the increase in the food resources that HE gave you. Therefore, you tithed on blessings God gave you from the things HE taught you to tithe against. [v22]

> *"To Tithe" meant worshipping God and feeding HIS people. It did not mean giving 10% of one's gross income to a church, which is apostasy. Edward*

To tithe the firstborn of your flocks or herds meant that out of every 10 newborn animals, you were to give 1 as a tithe. Ergo, you did not tithe from the existing herd or flock, but only on the increase in that herd or flock that God gave you.

Tithing never involved giving money.

Tithing was all about learning to fear and worship the LORD your God and to provide food for HIS people. God's instructions do mention the word "money." *Listen carefully to God's instruction.*

The word "money" is mentioned in the context of transporting your tithe to a place where God would have you consume it. And, what are you to do with your tithe money?

> **God says: "And you shall spend that money on whatever your heart desires: for oxen or sheep, for wine ..." [v26]**

A complete discussion of the tithe lie is not possible in this chapter. However, you can find a comprehensive discussion of the tithe in Chapter 17 of the *Book of Edward* found on the Internet at http://www.bookofedward.org/.

> **"For I am the LORD, I do not change; therefore you are not consumed, O sons of Jacob. Yet from the days of your fathers you have gone away from MY ordinances and have not kept them. Return to ME, and I will return to you," Says the LORD of hosts. "But you said, 'In what way shall we return?' " Malachi 3:6-7**

Immediately proceeding *"Will a man rob God?"* — we see that God is talking to the nation of Judah. The people of Judah did not obey God's ordinances on tithing. As a result, God's storehouse lacked food and the Levites did not give a *heave offering*. This was a "tenth of the tithe" [Numbers 18:26].

The message in Malachi 3:8-10 is clearly directed to the Hebrew people in Judah. Immediately following Malachi 3:8-10 is:

> **"And I will rebuke the devourer for your sakes, so that he will not destroy the fruit of your ground, nor shall the vine fail to bear fruit for you in the field," says the LORD of hosts; "And all nations will call you blessed, for you will be a delightful land," Says the LORD of hosts [God Almighty]. Malachi 3:11**

God instructs Judah through the prophet Malachi to obey the tithe ordinances and bring the tithe **"that there may be food in My house" [v10].** God's *food* message is *then* reinforced by His words: **"I will rebuke the devourer" [v11].** Ergo, God will provide great harvests for Judah if they obeyed Him.

Note: I believe the Hebrews staggered their tithe so the storehouse of food for those in need was filled every year.

Man's Tithe Instructions

Tithe preachers teach four lies in an appeal to our emotions of love, fear and greed.

1. **The tithe applies to everyone.**
   a. **False** – It *applied* only to Jews.
   b. Ask a Rabbi if Jews tithe today.

2. **God requires you to give 10% of your income to the church as a tithe.**
   a. **False** – It had nothing to do with giving money. It was only about food.

3. **God will curse you if you do not tithe.**
   a. **False** – Tithing is of the law and *ironically* Paul teaches that the exact opposite is true in Galatians 3:10. "Cursed is everyone who does not continue … to do all things [written in the book of the law].

4. **God will make you rich if you tithe.**
   a. **False** – Tithing *is* now a curse!

Some people think that godliness is a path to riches, but they are greatly deceived.

> **"Men of corrupt minds and destitute of the truth, who suppose that godliness is a means of gain. From such withdraw yourself. Now godliness with contentment is great gain. For we brought nothing into this world and it is certain we can carry nothing out. And having food and clothing, with these we shall be content. But those who desire to be rich fall into temptation and a snare, and into many foolish and harmful lusts, which drown men in destruction and perdition. For the love of money is a root of all kinds of evil, for which some have strayed from the faith in their greediness, and pierced themselves through with many sorrows. But you, O man of God, flee these things and pursue righteousness, godliness, faith, love, patience, gentleness." 1 Timothy 6:5-11**

Today's Tithe Essence

The essence of today's tithe teaching is a *give to get* message taught to people who are ignorant of Scripture and who value their preacher's words over the words of God. These are intellectually lazy people who are emotionally programmed against God's Word. Verily I say they are truly deceived.

As a result, many tithe preachers live lives of luxury even renting hotel rooms for $10,000 per night, according to one documentary. Many drive expensive cars, own private jets and multiple homes in luxury locations, all while teaching their flocks that each of them can also live lives of luxury, like they do, *just* by tithing [to them]!

The tithe *pitch* is an effective money-raising tool, because it appeals to the raw emotions of love and fear. Then, it couples those two emotions with that of greed and its inherent desire for material things and wealth.

There is no doubt that tithing is an appeal to human emotions and that it can cause many to be led astray, seeking friendship with the world and easy money!

The *pitch* is as basic as *the love of God*, the *fear of HIS curse*, and the idea that *HE wants to give you all that your heart desires*. This is a very seducing message to those ignorant of God's Word. And, any teacher who perverts God's Word by teaching the tithe can reinforce the tithe message with countless Scriptures.

> **"The blessing of YAHWEH is what brings riches;**
> **to this, hard toil has nothing to add."**
> **Proverbs 10:22 (NJB)**

Proverbs says it is God's blessings that will bring riches, not tithing. Even this verse can be twisted. Yet, in the face of the entire tithe lie come the words of Jesus Christ to his disciples. Let's now go back to where I started this chapter, the words of Jesus Christ.

What Jesus Taught

> **Jesus Christ sent his disciples out without any money, and they lacked nothing! How could that be? Think carefully about what Christ has taught us in this regard, and reflect on the Scriptures I cited on the cover page of this chapter for a little while.**

Ready to move on? It's quite a contrast, isn't it? Christ says we do not need money to be his disciple and an effective servant of God. Yet, many preachers now say they cannot be effective without tithes and offerings. Without money, how can we build a Church?

Do you believe Jesus or the tithe preacher? There is no contest here, is there? You *need* to accept the words of God and His Son over any teacher.

That includes me, if you should ever find His Word contradicting what I say. Let me tell you a secret. I firmly knew that the *offering* referred to in Malachi 3:8-10 was the *heave offering* that God required of the Levites. Remember, I taught you that it was "a tenth of the tithe." What you don't know is that I had actually taken it out, as I forgot the proof Scripture. I reasoned that if I couldn't provide a proof for you, this statement had to be deleted. However, God brought back to my memory Numbers 18:26, exactly where He gave the Levites these *heave* instructions.

It was important to me that you know this was an offering from the Levites that God referred to and not something more required of the people who were to tithe at the time.

The merchants of tithing would teach this as a second tithe to indicate God wants even more from you. However, it is God who called it "a heave offering" and defined it as "a tenth of the tithe." Well, back to Jesus.

Jesus talked about money a lot in the New Testament. One instance is in Matthew chapter 19. Remember the rich man? We read ...

> **Jesus said: "And again I say to you, it is easier for a camel to go through the eye of a needle than for a rich man to enter the kingdom of God." Matthew 19:24**

You might think Jesus is telling the rich young ruler that he won't get into heaven, but that is not true. Jesus already confirmed to him that he was assured of eternal life, because he obeyed the Ten Commandments. See Matthew 19:17-19. However, the rich young ruler asked, "What am I lacking?"

> **Jesus replied, "If you want to be perfect, go, sell what you have and give to the poor, and you will have treasure in heaven; and come, follow me."**
> **Matthew 19:21**

You might ask, "Why didn't Jesus tell him to bring the money into *his* ministry?"

Isn't that what a tithe preacher might say? Yes, it is. Bring in the cash, brother! But Jesus had a different standard by which to build his Church. And while I am on that thought, how should a church get built today? Free will offerings should build it!

To quote one scholar: "The old covenant society which Moses established at Mount Sinai, whether religious or secular, was supported (at first) simply by free will contributions. This is precisely the way the Christian Church was financed at first."

Jesus knew something that modern tithe preachers don't know. Money *is* a master!

> **Jesus said: "No one can serve two masters; for either he will hate the one and love the other, or else he will be loyal to the one and despise the other. You cannot serve [both] God and mammon [money]." Matthew 6:24**

Jesus knew that the rich young ruler served a master called money, even though he had assurance of eternal life. Jesus' statement about how difficult it is for the rich to enter the kingdom reflects the fact that money is a power that exerts control over our thoughts and can be a powerful master of our lives.

How do you change masters? Give all the wealth away and follow Jesus Christ. In the process, you walk away from the things of this earth and focus on the things of heaven.

When you walk away from the things of this world, you become a true servant of God. Your focus is on stewardship and not on the ownership of physical things, where money is *truly* a master that controls one's thoughts and greatly influences one's thinking.

> **"Do not love the world or the things in the world. If anyone loves the world, the love of the FATHER is not in him." 1 John 2:15**

In the Beatitudes, Jesus says:

> **"But woe to you who are rich, for you have received your consolation [while on the earth]."**
> **Luke 6:24**

Jesus knew money can buy a lot of things, but without it you have to trust in God to get the job done that HE wants you to do. This doesn't mean you won't have any money to work with. It means that God is the one you look to for resources, not the banker or any other human. It is HE that brings you what you need.

Tithing has become a lie used by Satan's ministers of righteousness to extract money, to lead us astray, to make us friends of the world, and make us an enemy of God. So, what are some sound biblical principles of giving that we can practice today? That is the final area I will address in this chapter. How should we give today? How do we give to God?

Seven Giving Principles

1. You choose the standard for receiving.

    "Give, and it will be given to you: Good measure, pressed down, shaken together, and running over will be put into your bosom. For with the same measure that you use, it will be measured back to you." Luke 6:38

2. Give bountifully.

3. Give with a purpose in your heart.

4. Do not give out of necessity.

5. Be a cheerful giver.

    "He who sows sparingly will also reap sparingly, and he who sows bountifully will also reap bountifully, so let each one give as he purposes in his heart, not grudgingly or [out] of [some] necessity for God loves a cheerful giver." 2 Corinthians 9:6-7

6. Do your good deeds and giving in secret.

    "But when you do your charitable deed, do not let your left hand know what your right hand is doing, that your charitable deed [or giving] may be in secret; and your FATHER who sees [your gift] in secret will HIMSELF reward you openly." Matthew 6:3-4

7. Understand that God owns everything.

"But you have given no glory to the God in whose hands are your breath itself and all your fortunes." Daniel 5:23

"For every beast of the forest is MINE, and the cattle on a thousand hills, I know all the birds of the mountains, and the wild beasts of the field *are* MINE. If I were hungry, I would not tell you; for the world *is* MINE, and all its fullness."
Psalms 50:10-12

Giving Directly To God

Do these six things to give directly to God.

1. Feed the hungry.
2. Give drink to the thirsty.
3. Take in the stranger.
4. Clothe the naked.
5. Visit the sick.
6. Go to those in prison.

"Come, you blessed of my FATHER, inherit the kingdom prepared for you from the foundation of the world: for I was hungry and you gave me food; I was thirsty and you gave me drink; I was a stranger and you took me in; I was naked and you clothed me; I was sick and you visited me; I was in prison and you came to me. ... In as much as you did it to one of the least of these my brethren you did it to me [and to my FATHER]."
Matthew 25:34-40

The Unfaithful

> Jesus said: " 'Well done good and faithful servant; [since] you were faithful over a few things, I will make you [a] ruler over many things.' And Jesus said: 'He who is faithful in what is least is faithful also in much; and he who is unjust in what is least is unjust also in much. Therefore if you have not been faithful in [what is] unrighteous [money], who will commit to your trust the true riches [of heaven]? And if you have not been faithful in what is another man's, who will give you what is your own?' " Apostle Edward

Bible References: Matthew 25:21; Luke 16:10-12

The Unfaithful Contents

	Page
Jesus On Faithfulness	161
Faithful In Small Things	163-164
Cheap Grace	164-165
Costly Grace	165-168
Costly Grace Scripture	169-171
Discussion	171-172
Salvation Lost	173-174
The Unfaithful Rejected	174
True Belief	175-176
Faithful - Unfaithful	176
Edward's Conclusion	177-178

Faithful In Small Things

Jesus teaches we *must* be faithful in the smallest of things, especially when in private and no one is around to observe if we are being unfaithful. It means we are:

1. Faithful over a few things.

2. Faithful in the least of things.

3. Faithful in simple things.

4. Faithful in the use of money.

5. Faithful in what belongs to another.

You might think that this is easy to do, but it is not if you are not guided by the Spirit of God. Putting off the old man and putting on the new man and learning to walk in the Spirit is what you need to do to accomplish this. It is God's Spirit that gives you the strength to walk by HIS ways and not man's.

Jesus also taught us to be faithful until our death if we want to receive a crown of life.

> **"Do not fear any of those things which you are about to suffer. Indeed, the devil is about to throw some of you into prison, that you may be tested, and you will have tribulation ten days. Be faithful until [your own] death, and I will give you the crown of life." Revelation 2:10**

How strong is your faith? Faithful unto death?

When Jesus taught us to be faithful until our own death, it was with the knowledge that many of us [if not most believers] would experience severe testing, tribulation, and/or maybe even torture.

So, the question becomes, will you die for your faith? If not, you do not have the kind of faith that God requires. And, you may not be faithful even in the smallest of things. If this is you, it is *cheap grace* that you have. Or, it is *cheap grace* that has been sold to you by a church that is no longer faithful to God's Holy Word.

Cheap Grace

"*Cheap grace* is the deadly enemy of our Church. We are fighting today for costly grace. Cheap grace means grace sold on the market like cheapjacks' wares. [Cheapjacks were sellers of inferior or cheapened goods].

The sacraments, the forgiveness of sin, and the consolations of religion are thrown away at cut [rate] prices. Grace is represented as the Church's inexhaustible treasury, from which she showers blessings with generous hands, without asking questions or [by] fixing limits. Grace without price; grace without cost! The essence of grace, we suppose, is that the account [for our sins] has been paid in advance; and, because it has been paid, everything can be had for nothing.... [45]" Note: Bracketed numbers in discussion reference pages in Dietrich Bonhoeffer's *Cost of Discipleship*.

"Cheap grace means grace as a doctrine, a principle, [or] a system."

"It means forgiveness of sins proclaimed as a general truth, the love of God taught as the Christian *conception* of God. An intellectual assent to that idea is held to be [in and] of itself sufficient to secure remission of sins."

"In such a Church the world finds a cheap covering for its sins; no contrition [remorse or repentance] is required, still less any real desire [of people] to be delivered from sin. Cheap grace therefore, amounts to a denial of the living word of God, in fact, a denial of the Incarnation of the word of God. [45-46]

Cheap grace means the justification of sin without the justification of the sinner. Grace alone does everything [the theologians] say, and so everything can remain as it was before. *'All for sin could not atone.'* Well, then, let the Christian live like the rest of the world, let him model himself on the world's standards in every sphere of life, and not presumptuously aspire to live a different life under grace from his old life under sin...."

"Cheap grace is the grace we bestow on ourselves. Cheap grace is the preaching of forgiveness without requiring repentance, Baptism without church discipline, Communion without confession.... Cheap grace is grace without discipleship, grace without the cross, grace without Jesus Christ, living [and dwelling inside us]." [47]

Costly Grace

"*Costly grace* is the treasure hidden in the field; for the sake of it a man will gladly go and sell all that he has. It is the pearl of great price to buy which the merchant will sell all his goods [for]. It is the kingly rule of Christ, for whose sake a man will pluck out [his] eye [if it] causes him to stumble [sin], it is the call of Jesus Christ at which the disciple leaves his nets and follows him."

"Costly grace is the gospel which must be sought again and again and again, the gift which must be asked for, the door at which a man must knock. Such grace is costly because it calls us to follow, and it is grace because it calls us to follow Jesus Christ."

"It is costly because it costs a man his life, and it is grace because it gives a man the only true life. It is costly because it condemns sin, and grace because it justifies the sinner. Above all, it is costly because it cost God the life of his Son: 'ye were bought at a price,' and what has cost God much cannot be cheap for us [or our souls].

Above all, it is grace because God did not reckon his [human] Son too dear a price to pay for our life, but delivered him up for us. Costly grace is the incarnation of [the Word of God through the human flesh of HIS *only* begotten Son Jesus Christ]."

"Costly grace is the sanctuary of God; it has to be protected from the world, and not thrown to the dogs. It is therefore, the living word, the Word of God, which HE speaks as it pleases HIM. Costly grace confronts us as a gracious call to follow Jesus. It comes as a word of forgiveness to the broken spirit and the contrite heart. Grace is costly because it compels a man to submit [himself] to the yoke of Christ and follow him; it is grace because Jesus says: 'My yoke is easy and my burden is light.' "

"On two separate occasions Peter received the call [from Jesus]: 'Follow me.' It was the first and last word Jesus spoke to his disciple (Mark 1:17; John 21:22). A whole life lies between these two calls. The first occasion was by the lake of Gennesareth, [Sea of Galilee] when Peter left his nets and his craft and followed Jesus at his word. The second occasion is when the Risen Lord [Jesus] finds [Peter] back again at his old trade."

"Once again it is by the lake of Gennesareth, and once again the call is [to]: 'Follow me.' Between the two calls lay a whole life of discipleship in the following of Christ. Half way between them comes Peter's confession, when he acknowledged Jesus as the Christ [the Son of God sent by HIM] ... [48]"

"It was the grace of Christ himself, now prevailing upon the disciple to leave all and follow him, now working in him that confession which to the world must sound like the ultimate blasphemy, now inviting Peter to the supreme fellowship of martyrdom for the Lord he had denied, and thereby forgiving him all his sins. In the life of Peter, grace and discipleship are [totally] inseparable. [Apostle Peter] had received the grace which costs; [the costly grace]." [49]

Peter received the costly grace!

"As Christianity spread, and the Church became more secularized, this realization of the costliness of grace gradually faded. The world was Christianized, and grace became its common property. [Grace] was to be had at [a very] low cost..." [49]

The above discussion on *cheap grace* and *costly grace* are from Dietrich Bonhoeffer's book titled *The Cost of Discipleship*. This discussion is on the Internet at http://www.crossroad.to/Persecution/Bonhoffer.html. Again, bracketed numbers are pages in his book.

Dietrich Bonhoeffer suffered death at the hands of the Nazis during World War II. Before dying for his faith, he came to the spiritual conclusion that unless one was willing to die for his or her faith, then that faith was based on *cheap grace* and would be found lacking before God.

"Verily I say unto you, such a faith is no faith at all!" Edward

Bonhoeffer also said: "Both modern liberal theology and secular totalitarianism hold pretty much in common that the message of the Bible has to be adapted more or less, to the requirements of a secular world. [That is why it is]

No wonder, therefore, that the process of debasing Christianity [with] liberal theology led, in the long run, to a complete perversion and falsification of the [true] essence of Christianity...." [30]

"A Christian must be prepared, if necessary, to offer his life for this [his/her faith]. Thus all kinds of secular totalitarianism which force man to cast aside his religious and moral obligations to God and subordinate [HIS] laws of justice and morality to the State [and its government or secular beliefs] are incompatible with [a true] conception of [Christian] life..." [31]

"The life of the spirit is not that which shuns death and keeps clear of destruction: rather it endures death and in death it is sustained. It only achieves its truth in the midst of utter destruction." [33]

"In a modern dictatorship, however, with its subterranean ubiquity and all-embracing instruments of oppression, a revolt means certain death to all who support it. ... The future in modern society depends much more on the quiet heroism of the very few who are inspired by God. These few will greatly enjoy the divine inspiration and will be prepared to stand for the dignity of man and true freedom and to keep the law of God, even if it means martyrdom or death."

> ***Because they*** **"Do not look at the things which are seen, but at the things which are not seen. For the things which are seen are temporary, but the things that are not seen are eternal."**
> **2 Corinthians 4:17-18**
>
> **"Be doers of the Word, and not hearers only, deceiving yourselves." James 1:22**

Costly Grace Scriptures

"If you were of the world, the world would love its own. Yet because you are not of the world, but I chose you out of the world, therefore the world hates you. ... If they persecuted me they will also persecute you. ... Because they do not know HIM who sent me." John 15:19-21

"Do not be conformed to this world, but be transformed by the renewing of your mind, that you may prove what is that good and acceptable and perfect will of God." Romans 12:2

"We know that we are of God, and the whole world lies under the sway of the wicked one."
1 John 5:19

Verily I say to you that the "whole organized denominational Church" also lies under the sway of the wicked one! Edward

"Do not be unequally yoked together with unbelievers. For what fellowship has righteousness with lawlessness? And what communion has light with darkness? And what accord has Christ with Belial [the devil]? Or what part has a believer with an unbeliever? And what agreement has the temple of God with idols? For you are the temple of the living God.

As God has said: 'I will dwell in them and walk among them. I will be their God, and they shall be MY people.' "

"Therefore, 'Come out from among them and be separate,' says the LORD. 'Do not touch what is unclean, and I will receive you. I will be a FATHER to you, and you shall be MY sons and daughters,' Says the LORD ALMIGHTY."
2 Corinthians 6:14-18

"Come out of her, MY people, lest you share in her sins, and lest you receive of her plagues."
Revelation 18:4

"The time is coming that whoever kills you will think that he offers God service. And these things they will do to you because they have not known the FATHER nor [have they known] me."
John 16:2-3

"They think it strange that you do not run with them in the same flood of dissipation, speaking evil of you." 1 Peter 4:4

" 'Therefore prepare yourself and arise, and speak to them all that I command you. Do not be dismayed before their faces, lest I dismay you before them. For behold, I have made you this day a fortified city and an iron pillar, and bronze walls against the whole land— Against the kings... princes... priests, and against the people of the land. They will fight against you, but they shall not prevail against you. For I *am* with you,' says the LORD, 'to deliver you.' " Jeremiah 1:17-19

"Do not enter the path of the wicked, and do not walk in the way of evil. Avoid it, do not travel on it; turn away from it and pass on."
Proverbs 4:14

> "But know this, that in the last days perilous times will come: For men will be lovers of themselves, lovers of money, boasters, proud, blasphemers, disobedient to parents, unthankful, unholy, unloving, unforgiving, slanderers, without self-control, brutal, despisers of good, traitors, headstrong, haughty, lovers of pleasure rather than lovers of God, having a form of godliness but denying its power. And from such people turn away!" 2 Timothy 3:1-5

> "Yes, and all who desire to live godly in Christ Jesus will suffer persecution. But evil men and impostors will grow worse and worse, deceiving and being deceived. But you must continue in the things which you have learned."
> 2 Timothy 3:12-14

The above spiritual truths are different than what most churches teach. Sincere faith in God and His Son Jesus does come with a cost attached. In exchange for sincere faith, we obtain eternal life after our short earthly journey ends. The true believer sees him or her self in the context of heaven. This allows them to become steadfast even in the face of earthly persecution. Their spirits know they are of God and do not belong to the world.

Many New Testament letters are addressed "to the faithful" or to "those who are sincere in the faith" or to "like minded believers."

> **Paul writes: "To the saints who are in Ephesus [*name your city*], and [*who are*] faithful in Christ Jesus." Ephesians 1:1**

If you have not accepted God's costly grace, your faith will not be sincere. It's because you will not have the strength and courage that only comes from a true conviction.

The letters in the Bible are spiritual letters and instructions from God to His children. When you read it with your spirit engaged, you will get what God wants to give you. When you read it with only your mind, you won't get God's message.

The process of debasing Christianity, which Bonhoeffer observed in the early 1940s, has continued on since his death. Christianity no longer resembles the Church that Christ sent his apostles out to build. The Church was supposed to be filled with believers who understood the costly nature of grace and who had the strength to be faithful to God.

> **Jesus said: "But why do you call me 'Lord, Lord,' and do not do the things which I say?"**
> **Luke 6:46**

The issue of costly grace clearly stems from the requirement of God that we are obedient to His Word. Jesus relays this important fact in Luke when he poses the question: "Why call me Lord when you do not obey me?" He could also have asked: "Why are you unfaithful?" When faced with death itself, will you stand firm or will you renounce your faith? The requirement is to be "faithful even unto our own death" in order to receive our crown of life.

True faith is costly and may even result in death on a cross or by some other cruel means. That is what happened to Peter. What about you? Ready? Or, will you say, "Well, Peter made the choice to die on the cross; I don't have to." For Peter there was never even a consideration, because he received the costly grace from Christ.

Jesus could have asked: "Why are you unfaithful?"

Salvation Lost

The debasing of the Church has led to the belief by many that their salvation is secure and cannot be lost. Listen to God's Word.

> **"For if we sin *willfully* after we have received the knowledge of the truth, there no longer remains a sacrifice for sins, but a certain fearful expectation of judgment, and fiery indignation which will devour the adversaries. Anyone who has rejected Moses' law dies without mercy on the testimony of two or three witnesses.**
>
> **Of how much worse punishment, do you suppose, will he be thought worthy who has trampled the Son of God underfoot, counted the blood of the covenant by which he was sanctified a common thing, and insulted the Spirit of grace? For we know HIM who said, 'Vengeance is MINE, I will repay,' says the LORD.**
>
> **And again, 'The LORD will judge HIS people.' It is a fearful thing to fall into the hands of the living God." Hebrews 10:26-32**

Yes, your salvation is lost if you continue to willfully sin. To do so, means you are not only lawless in regards to God's Word, you are also unfaithful to HIS Word. Isn't it the same thing?

For now, you need to understand that both God and HIS Son Jesus Christ fully expect you to be faithful to their instructions. This does not mean you will be perfect. It means you fully grasp the issues of cheap grace, costly grace and that of a true conviction.

Jesus said: "If I had not come and spoken to them, they would have no sin, but now they have no excuse for their sin." John 15:22

"Whoever commits sin also commits lawlessness, and sin is lawlessness." 1 John 3:4

The Unfaithful Rejected

In John 15:22, Jesus states we have no excuse for our willful sin. Note: there is unknown sin and also unintentional sin that are covered by Jesus' blood. See the *Book of Edward Volume I: Matters of the Heart* for a detailed discussion on the issue of sin.

In 1 John 3:4, we learn that sin is defined as lawlessness. It means we are disobedient and is another way of stating unfaithfulness.

1 John 3:4 could also have read: "Whoever commits sin also commits unfaithfulness and sin is unfaithfulness." Apostle Edward

In Matthew 7:23, we learn that Jesus rejects all who call on his name who are lawless. Those who are called lawless are simply people who were unfaithful to God. They never received the costly grace and in effect were sold a spiritual bill of goods that was worthless.

> ## Ergo, Jesus Rejects Unfaithful Christians!

True Belief

Just what constitutes true belief? Is it being informed on a subject? Having extensive knowledge of a subject? I have done a lot of thinking about this and I have come to the conclusion that knowledge alone does not constitute belief. Further, that the old adage "knowledge is power" is a lie and falsehood.

It is *applied knowledge* that is power. For example, the doctor or nurse who lights up a cigarette to smoke doesn't really believe that smoking is harmful to their health. Do they? Of course not, they have knowledge in their heads about the health problems of smoking, but there is no true belief in their hearts. If there were true belief, they would have no problem stopping smoking. So, *it is* applied knowledge that contains true power. Only when we have a firm conviction in our souls will we actually apply the knowledge we know or have learned.

So, we need to take action on the knowledge we have in order for it to do anything for us. It's the same thing when we accept Jesus as our savior. If we fail to obey his teachings, we fail to activate the spiritual power God has available for us. We also demonstrate to God that our proclaimed faith is a falsehood and that we are insincere towards HIM. For if we truly believed, wouldn't we seek to learn all about God and obey God's Word?

> **Again, listen to Jesus. "But *why* do you call me 'Lord, Lord,' and do not do the things which I say?" Luke 6:46**
>
> **"But if, while we seek to be justified by Christ, we ourselves also are found sinners, is Christ therefore a minister of sin? Certainly not!"**
> **Galatians 2:20**

Some of you Christians do not have knowledge of God!

"Awake to righteousness, and do not sin; for some do not have knowledge of God. I speak this to your shame." 1 Corinthians 15:34

Faithful - Unfaithful

"Love the LORD, all you HIS saints! For the LORD preserves the faithful." Psalms 31:23

"MY eyes shall be on the faithful ... that they may dwell with ME." Psalms 101:6

"A faithful man will abound with blessings." Proverbs 28:20

"The integrity of the upright will guide them, but the perversity of the unfaithful will destroy them." Proverbs 11:3

"Because they were unfaithful to ME ... I hid MY face from them." Ezekiel 39:26

"And they were unfaithful to the God of their fathers." 1 Chronicles 5:25

"For the LORD brought Judah low ... [for Ahaz king of Israel] had been continually unfaithful to the LORD." 2 Chronicles 28:19

There are 16 verses in the New King James that use the word "unfaithful" and 86 verses that use the word "faithful." This is only a sampling of them. Yet, clearly God is focused on the positive. So, be faithful to God! Obey HIS Word and the teachings of HIS Son and you *will* see HIS eternal life.

Edward's Conclusion

God originally asked me to write seven street tracts for HIM and this chapter was the seventh. Then HE asked me to put it into book form. Yet, when I look back, God has had me writing about how the Church at large has become incredibly unfaithful to HIM. All of the chapters of this book reflect that unfaithfulness.

In message one, *The Invitation*, God had me show you Scripture that showed how the Church has lied about the nature of HIS salvation. Even denying HIS Word that salvation comes directly from HIM. Is salvation a small matter of faithfulness?

In message two, *The Messenger*, God had me show you Scripture that showed how the Church has lied about the nature of Jesus Christ, God's only human begotten Son. Even denying HIS Word that Christ is not God. Is this a small matter of faithfulness?

In message three, *The Message*, God had me show you Scripture that showed how the Church has failed to open the minds and hearts of people. Even denying HIS Word that salvation is deeper than mouthing Jesus. Is this a small matter of faithfulness?

In message four, *Law of Christ*, God had me show you Scripture that showed how the Church has lied about the nature of God's Law and what Christ has done in terms of increasing HIS righteousness *standard* for our behavior. Even denying HIS Word that the Law has not entirely been done away with. Is this a small matter of faithfulness?

In message five, *The Seven Spirits*, God had me show you Scripture that showed how the Church has lied about the nature of God HIMSELF through the invention of a pagan god called the Trinity. Even denying HIS Word that God has seven Spirits and not just one. Is this a small matter of faithfulness?

In message six, *The Tithe Lie*, God had me show you Scripture that showed how the Church has lied about the nature of tithing in the Old Testament. Even denying HIS Word that tithing is of the law and no longer required. Is raising money through a false doctrine on tithing a small matter of faithfulness?

In this seventh message, *The Unfaithful*, God had me show you Scripture that showed how the Church has lied about being faithful and now has a cheap grace doctrine that leads many to Hell. Even denying HIS Word that faithfulness is a requirement of salvation. Is this a small matter of faithfulness?

The contrast is astonishing. Christ has taught us to be faithful even in small things. Yet Orthodox Church doctrines are unfaithful in very huge things, leading believers astray and keeping them out of God's kingdom.

Therefore, orthodoxy has resulted in corrupt religious institutions just like the one Jesus castigated the scribes and Pharisees about. The Church keeps people out of heaven and most churches are now as unfaithful to God as the first institution Christ reprimanded.

> **Jesus told the religious leaders: "But woe to you, scribes and Pharisees, hypocrites! For you shut up the kingdom of heaven against men; for you neither go in yourselves, nor do you allow those who are entering to go in." Matthew 23:13**

"Woe to whoever keeps people out of God's kingdom, for HE will surely repay them for such unfaithfulness!" Apostle Edward

Appendix A
A Real Salvation Prayer

FATHER God, let everyone who utters this prayer of salvation unto YOU, with a sincere heart, immediately feel the presence of YOUR Holy Spirit and equip them with the internal strength of conviction to stand tall for YOUR righteousness at all costs and even unto their own human death. Verily I say that this is YOUR expectation of their [and my] sincere heart. The Apostle Edward

INSTRUCTIONS: Pray out loud and offer up to God Almighty outstretched arms and the following prayer, on your knees, in the privacy of your prayer closet [private room, alone], and with your sincere heart. Verily I say unto you that your soul will see eternal life in Heaven upon the death of your earthly body if your heart is sincere with God to the point that your behavior turns to righteousness. Mark down the time, date and place of this gift of your heart to God and feel free to share this moment of time when you made a commitment to walk in God's ways with HIS priorities over your life.

PRAY: Heavenly FATHER, the only ONE and True God. YOU, who are also the FATHER and the only ONE and True God of my brother Jesus Christ whom YOU sent down as a living human sacrifice for the sins of all the humans in this earthly realm and world, hear this prayer from my sincere heart. This prayer comes from within the bowels of my spirit-soul and I fully understand that this is a one-way decision of my heart.

FATHER, I believe in YOUR only human begotten Son Jesus Christ. I believe that YOU sent Christ down to this earth and that he became the human being Jesus Christ [Yashua] in the flesh just like the flesh I have. I believe he had bones like I do, flesh like I do and blood like I do. I believe that his body on the cross was no different than any other human body on the cross. I acknowledge Jesus Christ is the Son of God; he is not God.

FATHER, I believe that he only spoke what YOU told him to say and that he only did what YOU told him to do. I believe that he was the final and perfect blood sacrifice for the forgiveness of the sins of mankind. FATHER I believe that includes my sins.

LORD, I fully acknowledge that by accepting Jesus Christ as my personal savior and brother that I am inviting his perfect spirit into my life to share this earthly body with me. Along with his spirit, I understand that you will also give me YOUR Holy Spirit and that YOU also will dwell within me.

I believe that the end result of my sincere acceptance of this gift of YOUR Son is the Oneness that I will share with YOU and him. Christ has taught me that I might live in perfect Oneness, Peace and Joy with YOU and him. O LORD, this is truly the sincere desire of my heart. I no longer want to be spiritually alone.

Therefore, I accept the precious gift of YOUR Son Jesus Christ and I repent of my past sins and sincerely regret every thought, action, behavior or anything that was displeasing unto YOU. I understand that with the precious gift of YOUR Son, YOU expect me to live a righteousness life the rest of my days on this earth.

Such a life entails living up to YOUR expectations and obeying what YOU and YOUR Son taught us in Holy Scripture. LORD, I acknowledge that I cannot be perfect in and of myself. I realize that to be like Christ requires that I "practice" righteousness and that I avoid sin to the best of my ability. I acknowledge that to continue willfully to sin is a tacit rejection of the gift of Jesus.

I also acknowledge, FATHER, that there will be unintentional and unknown sins that will come in my life. I understand that YOU and

Christ will cover those types of sin and function as a guide in my life to keep me on the narrow path to Heaven.

FATHER, I acknowledge that YOUR Son is not a free pass on sins like so many Christians believe. Therefore, when I realize I have sinned against YOU in any way, I promise to confess that sin immediately and to keep a short list of my missteps with YOU. I know YOU are faithful to forgive under such conditions, but I also realize that if any life is filled with such confessions that it will be a testimony of an insincere heart. I recognize YOUR instructions in Ezekiel 18 and that Jesus has not altered YOUR criteria for punishing sinners. Therefore, keep me under YOUR wings O God and give me a pure heart unto YOU.

Having said this, FATHER, I pray that you will dwell within me and help me to be the man [or woman] that you want me to be. I ask all of this in the name of Jesus Christ whom I confess with my mouth that he came in the flesh as YOUR only begotten SON. I acknowledge with my heart that YOU expect righteousness, a new life with changed behavior; behavior that glorifies YOU.

FATHER, help me to be an instrument of YOUR will even as Christ was such an instrument. Let this day be the first day of the rest of my life and help me to put away all offensive behavior and sin, which YOU hate. In the name of YOUR only begotten and beloved human Son Jesus, I pray. AMEN

Date and Time of Prayer:_____

Place of Prayer: _____

I First Told: _____

_____

Testimony:_____

_____

_____

Appendix B
Baptism Doctrine

THE QUESTION

```
An Internet email writer asks Apostle Edward: "What is
your doctrine on baptism?  Do you believe that it is
necessary to be baptized in order to go to Heaven?"
```

Dear Seeker,

This is a very deep question. I will do my best to answer it faithfully in a way that honors God and HIS Holy Scripture.

DOCTRINE

I believe in baptism by immersion as an "outward expression of a new heart, which is now set aside for God." In effect, such a water baptism declares to all you know [and to the world] that you are indeed a part of God's kingdom [and you are indeed headed towards a heavenly kingdom].

COMMENTARY & STUDY

In Ephesians 4:5 we read: "There is one Lord, one faith, one baptism." However, in Acts 19:3-4 we see the question posed: "Into what then were you baptized?" The answer: "Into John's baptism." John's baptism was one of "repentance for the remission of sins." See Mark 1:4. Explicit in Acts 19:3-4 is the reality that there was more than one type of baptism.

John the Baptist offered the proposition of a "real God, Heaven and Hell and thus a real reason for sincere repentance" to the people. It is clear in God's Word that any such sincere repentance [of the heart] would yield salvation or eternal life. Thus baptism, in this instance by John, leads to eternal life in Heaven.

John's baptism is not well understood in Christianity, which has perverted the intent of God's Holy Word and the Gospel of Christ. However, Ephesians 4:5 refers to another and second baptism. It is the baptism of Romans 6:4: "Therefore we were buried with him [Christ Jesus] through baptism into death, that just as Christ was raised from the dead by the glory of the FATHER, even so we should walk in newness of life."

Anyone who accepts Jesus Christ "in their heart" has indeed accepted the reality of God and has achieved a baptism of the Holy Spirit [a baptism unto death and resurrection in Christ]. This results in the indwelling of God, HIS Son and the Spirit of truth that allows you to walk in a "newness of life." It gives you the strength to stand tall, firm and unwavering for God's truth in the simple language of the Holy Bible. Such a person now manifests the kingdom of God from within outward into the world around them. Even though, at this point, there may not have been a water baptism.

Baby baptism means virtually nothing because at the age of accountability [about 12 years old], each individual will have to make his or her choice as to which side he or she is on. No one can make this choice for another soul.

It took 10 years, after God touched my heart, for me to get baptized by immersion. It was a wonderful moment in time for me as it had bothered my spirit for a long time. Perhaps out of the misdirection of Christian theology and not fully understanding God's Holy Word. Or, perhaps out of the desire of my heart to proclaim that "I belong to God." Or, perhaps out of verses like Acts 10:47 indicating I could be baptized "having already received the Holy Spirit" and Acts 8:37 since "I believed with all my heart."

The verse that was my spiritual testimony at the time of my water baptism was Acts 22:15-16: "For you will be HIS witness to all men of what you have seen and heard. 'And now why are you waiting? Arise and be baptized, and wash away your sins, calling on the name of the LORD.' "

And now, Edward, why are *you* waiting? I knew where my heart was and the book of Acts indicated to my spirit that it was a special privilege to get baptized by immersion having met all of God's 'heart' criteria to ... make an outward declaration of the faith that was inside of my heart!

CASE 1: Anyone who is baptized by immersion and repents unto God for his or her sins will be saved and enter into eternal life. Assuming they then walk a godly life. This is true even without them having accepted Christ since they have already "accepted God."

CASE 2: Anyone who accepts Christ accepts God and, if Christ is within them, they will walk in the newness of life through a baptism of the Holy Spirit. This is true even if they have not been water baptized by immersion. Assuming they then walk a godly life and are "truly repentant."

This baptism doctrine fully recognizes all of God's Word. When you study Ezekiel 18, you will understand Case 1. It is consistent with the Gospel of Christ, which is "to repent and be saved." Many Christians no longer have this perspective of repentance. It is a critical part of salvation. Repentance leads to righteousness. Righteous people belong to God!

Case 2 is also consistent with God's Word. God has offered us a different dynamic with HIS Son. Plus, HE has provided some spiritual help that we can internalize through Christ: the indwelling of HIS Holy Spirit abundantly.

Case 2 is consistent with Romans 10:9-10, which spells out what is required for salvation through Christ. Water baptism is not a part of the criteria Paul outlined, because his criteria, results in a baptism of your spirit-soul and also a committed heart.

As such, you have accepted God's Spirit via Christ. It is a 'Spirit' baptism. Both baptisms require the total surrendering of your heart and life in obedience to God. Do either and HIS Spirit will confirm to your spirit-soul that you are indeed saved unto eternal life. *The Apostle Edward*

"THE LORD OUR GOD IS [ONLY] ONE!" Deuteronomy 6:4

Appendix C
Thomas' Exclamation

> "Then [Jesus] said to Thomas, 'Put your finger here and see my hands, and bring your hand and put it into my side, and do not be unbelieving, but believe.' Thomas answered and said to him, 'My Lord and my God!' Jesus said to him, 'Have you come to believe because you have seen me? Blessed are those who have not seen and have believed.' Now Jesus did many other signs in the presence of (his) disciples that are not written in this book. But these are written that you may (come to) believe that Jesus is the Messiah, the Son of God, and that through this belief you may have life in his name." John 20:27-31 (NAB)
>
> Thomas answered and said to Jesus: "My Lord and my God!" v28

So desperate are Trinitarian believers to rationalize the false doctrine of the trinity, that they will take verses out of context, ignore prior teachings of Jesus and in the process, make our Lord Jesus Christ a complete liar. A mere eleven verses earlier we read:

> Jesus said to her, "Stop holding on to me, for I have not yet ascended to the Father. But go to my brothers and tell them, 'I am going to my FATHER and your FATHER, to my God and your God.' " John 20:17 (NAB)

In our modern vernacular, Thomas' statement would be most properly interpreted as meaning, "O' my God, its true, its Jesus!" Thomas does not say: "Jesus is God!" as so many think he has. Did Jesus lie to us eleven verses earlier in the same chapter? If not, then how can anyone teach or believe Apostle Thomas would verbalize such apostasy? If you continue reading after Thomas' exclamation, we see that "these words are written" in the book of John so that you may ...

>**"Come to believe that Jesus is the Messiah, the Son of God!" v31**

Or how about, **"Peace to you! As the FATHER has sent me, I also send you." v21**

And, then Jesus breathed on them saying, **"Receive the Holy Spirit." v22**

Thomas was not with them when the other Apostles received the Holy Spirit or the Spirit of Truth. However, eight days later, Thomas was present when Jesus returned. This is the context for Thomas' exclamatory statement in John chapter 20. Yet, there is so much more context when it comes to what the apostles were taught. Jesus made it plain to all of his disciples that he was not God.

In Jesus' prayers to God [earlier in John 17], he told our FATHER that he had taught the disciples HIS Word and that they remained faithful to God's Word. Listen carefully to the conversation that Jesus had with his God [the FATHER] concerning what he had taught all of the disciples.

> **Jesus, while praying to God said: "I revealed YOUR name to those whom YOU gave me out of the world. They belonged to YOU, and YOU gave them to me, and they have kept YOUR word. Now they know that everything YOU gave me is from YOU, because the words YOU gave to me I have given to them, and they accepted them and truly understood that I came from YOU, and they have believed that YOU sent me."**
> **John 17:6-8 (NAB)**

So, Jesus told God that his disciples:

A) Had God's name [Yahweh] revealed to them;

B) Had kept God's Word;

C) Knew God gave everything to Jesus;

D) Accepted Jesus' teachings as words from God;

E) Truly understood Jesus was the Son of God, the Christ, who came from God;

F) Believed that God [Yahweh] had sent Jesus.

I feel a righteous indignation swelling up into my body and I feel like literally *SCREAMING AT THE TOP OF MY LUNGS*, "Why do people make Jesus a liar by claiming 'Thomas worshipped Jesus and identified him as God?' " The Apostle Thomas knew better than to do such a thing! How do we know? Jesus teaches us that the apostles "knew who God was!" I could go deeper and cite many other verses, but what is the point? Isn't this enough? Can't you simply accept the teachings of Jesus as truth?

> "If anyone teaches otherwise and does not consent to wholesome words, even the words of our Lord Jesus Christ, and to the doctrine which is according to godliness, he is proud, knowing nothing, but is obsessed with disputes and arguments over words, from which come envy, strife, reviling, evil suspicions."
>
> 1 Timothy 6:3-4 (NKJV)

I tell you to accept the teachings of our Lord Jesus Christ and stop making him out to be a liar by contradicting him or twisting his words. Meditate on 1 Timothy 6:3-4 if you don't get it. You must accept the teachings of Jesus if you want to understand Scripture. If you don't agree and consent to the teachings of Jesus, "you know nothing!" Surely God will repay every teacher who misleads others about the teachings of our Lord Jesus Christ.

Remember John 20:17?

Where Jesus identifies our God?

Then why not simply ...

Accept Jesus' teaching that the identity

Of his and our <u>God</u>, *is actually just*

The <u>FATHER</u>!

Thomas' Exclamation

Notes

1 — (1611) *The Authorized King James Version* (KJV). Comment: The KJV is in the public domain in the United States and is therefore freely used and quoted by many people. Also, anyone can freely publish the KJV Bible.

2 — (1982) *Holy Bible, New King James Version* (NKJV). Nashville, Tennessee: Thomas Nelson, Inc. Copyright © 1979, 1980, 1982. Comment: The NKJV is an update to the KJV and closely parallels the KJV text. In the author's opinion, the NKJV Bible is an excellent way to enjoy the KJV without getting entangled in trying to comprehend its archaic and outdated English. See chapter 6 for a discussion of the errors found in the KJV.

3 — (1987) *The Amplified Bible* (AMP). La Habra, California: The Zondervan Corporation and the Lockman Foundation.

4 — (1901) *American Standard Bible* (ASB).

5 — (1970) *New American Standard Bible* (NASB). New York, NY: Catholic Book Publishing Company. Copyright by the Confraternity of Christian Doctrine, Wash. DC.

6 — (1977) *New American Standard Bible* (NASB). New York, NY: Catholic Book Publishing Company. Copyright by the Confraternity of Christian Doctrine, Wash. DC.

7 — (1949) *Bible In Basic English* (BBE). Cambridge: The University Press, 1949. This Bible is in the Public Domain. It is downloadable and can be read online at http://www.o-bible.com/bbe.html.

8 — (1995) *Contemporary English Version* (CEV), Copyright by The American Bible Society, 1865 Broadway, New York, NY 10023.

9 — Darby, John Nelson. Public Domain, 1833. *Darby Bible* (DB).

10 — (1957) *New Catholic Edition of the Holy Bible* (Douay-Rheims), Copyright by Catholic Book Publishing Company, New York. *Note: the Old Testament is the Confraternity - Douay Version. The New Testament Confraternity Edition is a revision of the Challoner-Rheims Version.*

11— (1917) *Book of Enoch* (ENO). Richard Laurence 1883 Edition.

12 — (2001) *English Standard Version* (ESV), Copyright by Crossway Bibles, a division of Good News Publisher. Adapted from the Revised Standard Version of the Bible, copyright Division of Christian Education of the National Council of the Churches of Christ in the U.S.A.

13 — (1599) *The Geneva Bible* (GEN) is in the public domain and available online.

14 — (1978) *Good News Bible* (GN). Copyright by American Bible Society. New York: Thomas Nelson Publishers. Aka *"The Bible in Today's English Version;" or, "Today's English Version."*

15 — (1978) *Good News Bible; with Deuterocanonicals/Apocrypha* (GNA). Copyright by American Bible Society. New York: Thomas Nelson Publishers. Aka *"The Bible in Today's English Version; with Apocrypha."*

16 — (1995) *God's Word* (GW). Copyright by the Nations Bible Society. Database © 1997 by NavPress Software at www.WORDsearchBible.com.

17 — Mamre, Mechon (2002) *The Hebrew Bible in English according to the JPS 1917 Edition; HTML Version* (HEB). Internet: http://www.mechon-mamre.org.

18 — (1999) *Holman Christian Standard Bible* (HOL). Copyright © 2003, 2002, 2000, 1999 by Holman Bible Publishers.

19 — (1986) *International Children's Bible* (ICB). Copyright © 1986, 1988, 1999 by Tommy Nelson™, a division of Thomas Nelson, Inc.

20 — Berlin, Adele and Brettler, March Zvi (Editors) (2004) *Jewish Study Bible* (JSB). Jewish Publication Society, Tanakh Translation. Oxford, NY: Oxford University Press.

21 — (1971) *The Living Bible* (LIV). Wheaton, Illinois: Tyndale House Publishers.

22 — (1996) *Holy Bible, New Living Translation* (NLT). Wheaton, Illinois: Tyndale House Publishers.

23 — (1988) *Microbible* (MB). Copyright by Ellis Enterprises, Inc.

24 — (2003) *The Message* (MES). Copyright by Eugene H. Peterson, NavPress Publishing Group, P.O. Box 35001, Colorado Springs, CO 80935

25 — (1988) *Morris Literal Translation* (MLT). Copyright by Ellis Enterprises, Inc., Oklahoma City, OK. See "The Bible Library" software.

26 — Moffatt, James A. R. (1922, 1924, 1925, 1926, 1935, 1950, 1952 and 1954). *The Bible: James Moffatt Translation* (MOF). Final Edition used and Copyrighted in 1994 by Kregel Publications, Grand Rapids, Michigan.

27 — (1991) *New American Bible* (NAB), Copyright by the Confraternity of Christian Doctrine, 3211 Fourth Street, N.E., Washington D.C. 20017

28 — (2005) *The NET Bible, New English Translation*, Copyright 1996-2005, Biblical Studies Press, L.L.C., www.bible.org.

29 — (1984) *The Holy Bible, New International Version* (NIV). Copyright by International Bible Society. Published by Zondervan Bible Publishers.

30 — (1991) *The Holy Bible, New Century Version* (NCV). Aka "*The Everyday Bible.*" Dallas, Texas: Word Publishing. Comment: Excellent modern English translation.

31 — (1985) *The New Jerusalem Bible* (NJB). Copyright by Darton, Longman & Todd Ltd and Doubleday, a division of Bantam Doubleday Dell Publishing.

32 — (1958) *Phillips New Testament Bible* (PNT). Copyright held by Harper Collins. Copyright Administrator, The Archbishops' Council, Church House, Great Smith Street, London SW1P 3AZ, Tel (UK): 020 7898 1451; Fax (UK) 020 7898 1449; e-mail copyright@c-of-e.org.uk. On the web at http://www.ccel.org/bible/phillips/JBPNT.htm

33 — (1989) *The Revised English Bible* (REB). Copyright by Oxford University Press and Cambridge University Press. Comment: The Revised English Bible is a revision of The New English Bible.

34 — (1952) *Revised Standard Version* (RSV). Copyright by Division of Christian Education of the National Council of Churches of Christ in the United States of America. Zondervan Publishing House.

35 — (1989) *New Revised Standard Version* (NRSV). Copyright by Division of Christian Education of the National Council of Churches of Christ in the United States of America. Zondervan Publishing House.

36 — (1981) *Simple English Translation, New Testament* (SET). Copyright by International Bible Translators, Inc.

37 — Scherman, Nosson and Zlotowitz, Meir (General Editors). (1996) *The Stone Edition, Tanach* (TAN). Brooklyn, New York: Mesorah Publications, Ltd.

38 — (1988) *Transliterated Bible* (TB). Copyright by Ellis Enterprises, Inc.

39 — Webster, Noah. Public Domain, 1833. *Webster's Bible* (WEB).

40 — Wesley, John. Public Domain, 1755. *Wesley New Testament* (WES).

41 — Clarke, J. Public Domain, 1909. *Weymouth's New Testament* (WEY).

42 — Young, Robert. Public Domain, 1898. *Young's Literal Translation* (YLT).

Notice: Fair use under copyright laws are claimed for all the verses cited from the above bibles that are not in the public domain. Due to the scholarly nature of this religious book, the capitalization protocol deployed by its author to properly identify God in all Scripture, and the controversial nature of the trinity doctrine, no permissions have been sought from copyright holders. Readers are referred back to the original Bible works for the original capitalization of the words used within cited verses.

Scripture
Cross Reference

Scripture Cross Reference

1 Chronicles 5:25, 176

1 Corinthians 6:9-10, 115
1 Corinthians 8, 47
1 Corinthians 8:4-6, 47
1 Corinthians 8:6, vii, viii, 57
1 Corinthians 9:20-21, 101
1 Corinthians 9:21, 99, 101, 102
1 Corinthians 15:34, 93, 176

1 John 2:15, 55, 157
1 John 3:4, 174
1 John 3:5-8, 119
1 John 3:7, 95
1 John 4:3, 131
1 John 4:9, 39
1 John 5:3, 106
1 John 5:19, 169
1 John 5:20, 52, 136

1 Peter 1:21, 115
1 Peter 1:21-22, 73
1 Peter 1:22-23, 49
1 Peter 1:23, 49, 92
1 Peter 3:12, 114
1 Peter 4:4, 170
1 Peter 4:14, 132, 133

1 Timothy 1:7-8, 144
1 Timothy 6:3-4, 192
1 Timothy 6:5-11, 153

2 Chronicles 16:9, 49
2 Chronicles 28:19, 176

2 Corinthians 3:6-18, 108
2 Corinthians 4:17-18, 168
2 Corinthians 6:14-18, 170
2 Corinthians 9:6-7, 158

2 Esdras 8
2 Esdras 8:1, 8
2 Esdras 8:1-9:22, 8
2 Esdras 8:50, 8
2 Esdras 9:1-2, 9
2 Esdras 9:3-6, 9
2 Esdras 9:6, 11
2 Esdras 9:7-12, 10

2 John 7, 52

2 Peter 2:1, 16
2 Peter 2:12-17, 104
2 Peter 2:12-22, 104
2 Peter 2:15, 16, 19, 103
2 Peter 3:3, 15
2 Peter 3:9, 115

2 Thessalonians 1:8, 45, 68
2 Thessalonians 2:9-10, 84

2 Timothy 3:1-5, 171
2 Timothy 3:12-14, 171
2 Timothy 4:2, 110
2 Timothy 4:3-4, 144

Acts 2:38-39, 97
Acts 3:26, 71
Acts 8:37, 186
Acts 10:34, 32
Acts 10:34-35, 113
Acts 10:47, 186
Acts 17:11, 83
Acts 19:3-4, 185

Acts Continued
Acts 22:15-16, 187
Acts 26:17-18, 43

Colossians 2:16-17, 108

Daniel 5:23, 159

Deuteronomy 5:7, 136
Deuteronomy 5:12, 106
Deuteronomy 5:29, 134
Deuteronomy 6:4, 188
Deuteronomy 6:4-5, 130
Deuteronomy 6:6-9, 109
Deuteronomy 6:24-25, 134
Deuteronomy 12:32, 145
Deuteronomy 14:22-27, 149
Deuteronomy 14:22-29, 88, 147, 148
Deuteronomy 14:27-28, 149

Ecclesiastes 3:11, 112
Ecclesiastes 3:14, 113

Ephesians 1:1, 171
Ephesians 4:5, 185, 186

Exodus 16:23-26, 107
Exodus 31:15-16, 107
Exodus 34:7, 82
Exodus 35, 107

Ezekiel 14:14, 94
Ezekiel 18, 91, 187
Ezekiel 18:9, 93
Ezekiel 18:21, 94
Ezekiel 18:31, 94
Ezekiel 39:26, 176

Galatians 2:15-16, 108
Galatians 2:20, 175
Galatians 3:15-29, 108

Hebrews 2:17, 46
Hebrews 2:17-18, 89
Hebrews 5:9, 74, 93, 110
Hebrews 7:16-17, 46
Hebrews 9:10, 108
Hebrews 9:19-20, 80
Hebrews 10:26-32, 173
Hebrews 11:1, 42
Hebrews 11:6, 41

Isaiah 11:2, 131, 133
Isaiah 40:3-5, 64
Isaiah 43:10-11, 64, 92
Isaiah 44:22, 136

James 1:22, 168
James 2:20, 29
James 2:26, 29
James 3:1, 144
James 4:17, 111, 112, 144, 145

Jeremiah 1:17-19, 170
Jeremiah 4:1, 136
Jeremiah 24:7, 137
Jeremiah 29:13, 41
Jeremiah 31:33-34, 112

Joel 2:12, 137
Joel 2:32, 91, 93, 95, 137
Joel 3:5, 137

John 3:3, 49
John 3:7, 49
John 3:7-8, 49
John 3:16, 44
John 3:16, 3:36, 93

John Continued

John 3:36, 44, 46
John 4:23-24, 46
John 4:30, 71
John 4:34, 71
John 5:24, 36-37, 54, 65-71, 93
John 5:26, 65, 92-93
John 5:30, 1, 71
John 5:36, 1
John 5:37, 1
John 5:38, 1
John 6:29, 71
John 6:35-39, 66
John 6:38, 1, 72
John 6:39, 1
John 6:40, 1, 67
John 6:44, 1, 36, 37, 67
John 6:45, 36
John 6:54, 67
John 6:63, 55
John 6:63-64, 79
John 7:16, 54, 71, 72
John 7:18, 1
John 7:28, 1
John 7:29, 1
John 7:30, 1
John 8:16, 71
John 8:18, 1
John 8:26, 1
John 8:29, 1
John 8:42, 1
John 8:47, viii, 128
John 9:4, 71, 72
John 10:26, 1
John 11:42, 1
John 12, 70
John 12:44, 45, 73, 135
John 12:44, 45, 1
John 12:45, 73
John 12:48, 36, 37
John 12:48-39, 70
John 12:49, 71
John 12:50, 110
John 13:16, 72
John 13:16, 20, 71
John 14:6, 90, 91
John 14:17, 132, 133
John 14:23, 39
John 14:24, 70, 71, 72
John 14:28, 72
John 15:17, 110
John 15:19-21, 169
John 15:21, 71
John 15:22, 174
John 16:2, 14
John 16:2-3, 170
John 16:5, 71
John 16:23-24, 79, 80
John 16:24, 79
John 17, 190
John 17:1-3, 135
John 17:3, 54, 72, 128
John 17:3, 8, 18, 21, 71
John 17:6-8, 191
John 17:25, 71
John 20, 190
John 20:17, vii, viii, 45, 57, 68, 69, 70, 88, 128, 189, 192
John 20:21, 71
John 20:23, 94
John 20:27-31, 189
John 21:22, 166

Leviticus 16, 107
Leviticus 19:28, 117
Leviticus 23, 107
Leviticus 24, 107
Leviticus 25, 107

Luke 1:6, 97
Luke 4:18: 4:43, 71
Luke 4:43, 20, 52, 71

Luke Continued

Luke 6:24, 157
Luke 6:38, 158
Luke 6:46, 106, 172, 175
Luke 9:2-3, 141
Luke 9:48, 71
Luke 10:3-4, 141
Luke 13:3, 97
Luke 16:10-12, 161
Luke 22:35, 141

Malachi 2:7, 110
Malachi 3:6, 91, 102
Malachi 3:6-7, 151
Malachi 3:8-10, 143, 151, 155
Malachi 3:11, 151
Malachi 3:16-18, 53

Mark 1:4, 185
Mark 1:17, 166
Mark 2:27, 109

Matthew 4:10, 46, 74, 128
Matthew 4:17, 20, 96
Matthew 5:11-12, 30
Matthew 5:17, 106
Matthew 5:20, 51, 94
Matthew 5:21-22, 117
Matthew 5:27-28, 118
Matthew 5:38-39, 118
Matthew 5:43-44, 119
Matthew 5-7, 117
Matthew 6:3-4, 158
Matthew 6:6, 46
Matthew 6:24, 156
Matthew 7:21, 42, 95, 106
Matthew 7:21-23, vii, 11, 30, 36, 69
Matthew 7:23, 43, 102, 174
Matthew 9:13, 96

Matthew 10:40, 71
Matthew 11:15, 87
Matthew 12:8, 107
Matthew 13:9, 87
Matthew 13:10-19, 85
Matthew 13:13, 77
Matthew 13:20, 86
Matthew 13:20-21, 86
Matthew 13:22, 86
Matthew 13:23, 86
Matthew 13:43, 94
Matthew 15:3, 128
Matthew 15:24, 1
Matthew 17:5, ix
Matthew 18:6-7, 146
Matthew 19, 155
Matthew 19:17, 94
Matthew 19:17-19, 156
Matthew 19:21, 156
Matthew 19:24, 155
Matthew 21:31-32, 96
Matthew 21:33-40, 61, 63
Matthew 22:29, 144
Matthew 22:37-39, 111
Matthew 23:13, 178
Matthew 24, 2, 4, 5, 14, 24
Matthew 24:3, 1
Matthew 24:8, 8
Matthew 24:13, 17
Matthew 24:14, 18
Matthew 24:15, 21
Matthew 24:27, 22
Matthew 24:29, 22
Matthew 24:30, 22
Matthew 24:32-34, 23
Matthew 24:33, 23
Matthew 24:36-44, 23
Matthew 24:37, 23
Matthew 24:45-50, 24
Matthew 24:50, 24
Matthew 24-25, 2, 36
Matthew 25, 25, 29, 35

Matthew Continued

Matthew 25:14-30, 31
Matthew 25:21, 161
Matthew 25:21, 23, 31
Matthew 25:30, 31
Matthew 25:31-46, 32
Matthew 25:32-34, 32
Matthew 25:34-40, 159
Matthew 25:35-36, 33
Matthew 25:37-39, 33
Matthew 25:40, 33
Matthew 25:41-43, 34
Matthew 25:44, 34
Matthew 25:45, 34
Matthew 25:46, 34, 36, 37

Numbers 15, 107
Numbers 18:26, 155
Numbers 23:19, 129, 146

Philippians 2:12, 17

Proverbs 4:14, 170
Proverbs 10:22, 154
Proverbs 11:3, 176
Proverbs 28:20, 176

Psalms 1:6, 106
Psalms 3:8, 92
Psalms 30:5-6, 145
Psalms 31:23, 176
Psalms 46:10, 113
Psalms 50:10-12, 159
Psalms 50:23, 93
Psalms 101:6, 176

Revelation 1:4, 46, 121, 123
Revelation 1:4-5, 124
Revelation 1:5-6, 124

Revelation 1:8, 124, 125
Revelation 1:17-18, 125
Revelation 2:6, 103
Revelation 2:10, 163
Revelation 2:10-11, 17
Revelation 2:14, 103
Revelation 2:14-15, 103
Revelation 2:14-17, 103
Revelation 3:1, 127
Revelation 3:14, 46
Revelation 3:20-21, 39
Revelation 4:5, 127
Revelation 5:6, 127
Revelation 7:10, 65, 92
Revelation 7:11, 54
Revelation 14:7, 46
Revelation 18:4, 170
Revelation 22:11, 90
Revelation 22:15, 115, 145
Revelation 22:18-19, 145

Romans 1:4, 132, 133
Romans 1:18, 115
Romans 4:8, 93
Romans 6:4, 186
Romans 6:22, 93
Romans 7:25, 105
Romans 10:8-10, 50
Romans 10:9-10, 188
Romans 10:10, 35, 93
Romans 10:13, 95
Romans 10:17, 42ß
Romans 12:2, 169

Sirach 10:4-5, 13

Wisdom 5:2, 94

Zechariah 12:10, 132, 133

The Apostle Edward asks ... Are You Ready?

When he returns for souls, will Christ find you going about God's business? Will he find your spiritual light shining? If not, why? Do you even know why Christ stated those two salvation requirements?

There is an exodus from established churches by Christians who have found out that many churches no longer teach God's truth. The trend is worldwide and was the subject of a recent newsletter I received. These Christians read the Bible and compared what their church taught. They found that the Church supported many evil things that God abhors. In the process, they have asked themselves some fundamental spiritual questions:

- Can we support abortion if God abhors the shedding of innocent blood?

- Can we support Gay rights if God says homosexuality is abominable?

- Can we support a political party that seeks to excise God from everyday life?

- Can we support world friendship when it makes us God's enemy?

Christian mythology is rampant. The *Book of Edward* discusses the above and many other important issues that the Church is now confronted with.

Will you personally obey God's Word and the teachings of Jesus? If not, you are not saved. This book can reawaken your spirit and save your soul. At the very least, it will educate your heart.

I can remember the first experience in which I felt betrayed and confused by a pulpit teaching that did not line up and match what the word of God actually said. The basic choice you have, as a Christian, is whether you will adhere to God's Word or to the man made doctrines of your social group, your church, its hierarchy or its denomination.

There lies the main issue of salvation. You'll have to decide on God's Word if you want eternal life for in the end analysis you will be held accountable to His Word. Christians are leaving the established church and finding small fellowships or home churches as described in the New Testament. God has opened their eyes to His truth and if you read and study the Scriptures in this book, He will open your eyes.

Jesus said: "He who rejects me, and does not receive my words, has that which judges him; the word that I have spoken will judge him in the last day." John 12:48

If desired, you may write to me in care of Apostle Ministry, Inc. May your soul find the true salvation contained in the teachings of Jesus Christ. The Apostle Edward

Contact Apostle Edward

Apostle Edward's Contact Information

Reverend Edward G. Palmer
C/O Apostle Ministry, Inc.
18140 Zane Street NW, #410
Elk River, Minnesota 55330

Online Feedback Form
http://www.bookofedward.org/feedback.html

Online Tell-A-Friend Form
http://www.bookofedward.org/TAF-Form_1.html

Online Secure Donation Form
http://www.bookofedward.org/donation.html

Free Newsletter
www.bookofedward.org

> Do you want objective Scripture-based answers? Where Scripture itself speaks to you? Then, sign up for Apostle Edward's Free Online Newsletter. Email addresses will be validated. After you sign up, you will be asked to confirm your email.

http://www.bookofedward.org/

Tell-A-Friend!

**Seven End-Times
Messages From God**
http://www.sevenmessages.com

Trinity Dogma
http://www.trinitydogma.com

JVED Publishing

www.jvedpublishing.org

Apostle Edward also wrote the —
"Book of Edward: Christian Mythology"
http://www.bookofedward.org

Available Online And From All Book Stores Nationwide

You can buy the *Book of Edward* online in print form and from any bookstore including Amazon, Barnes & Noble, etc. or at http://www.bookofedward.org. If you buy Edward's four-volume set directly from Apostle Ministry, a free slipcase worth $59.95 will be sent to you at no charge. This slipcase is only available from Apostle Ministry, but it can be purchased if books are purchased elsewhere. You can also mail or fax your order by using the Order Form on the next page. All *Book of Edward*

e-Books and e-Chapters are fully searchable PDF files and are available online at http://www.bookofedward.org/esales.html. These PDF e-Book and e-Chapter files can also be ordered using the Order Form. They will be shipped to you on a CD.

Charitable Donations

Charitable donations to Apostle Ministry, Inc. are welcome and accepted. The funds received from your purchase of this book are used to support God's work. This includes buying bibles for Hindu families in India as well as supporting a ministry outreach program in India to reach unsaved souls. You can make a ministry donation online at http://www.bookofedward.org/donation.html.

Book of Edward
Mail & Fax Order Form

#	Item	Item Description	Price
1	0-9798833-0-9	Book of Edward - Volume I: Matters Of The Heart	$27.95
2	0-9768833-1-7	Book of Edward - Volume II: God Does Not Change	$27.95
3	0-9768833-2-5	Book of Edward - Volume III: Itching Christian Ears	$39.95
4	0-9768833-3-3	Book of Edward - Volume IV: Appendixes-Reference	$27.95
5	0-9768833-4-1	Book of Edward - Four Volume Set (Includes Slipcase)	$123.80
6	SLI-1	Slipcase	$59.95
7	CGI-1	Color Graphics Set One	$19.95
10	EBK-HC	God's Healing And Cancer - e-Book	$19.95
11	EBK-V1	Book of Edward – Volume I - e-Book	$19.95
12	EBK-V4	Book of Edward – Volume IV - e-Book	$14.95
13	ECH-8	e-Chapter 8 – Understanding God's Word	$9.95
14	ECH-9	e-Chapter 9 – Rationalization of Mankind	$9.95
15	ECH-10	e-Chapter 10 – The False Trinity Doctrine	$9.95
16	ECH-11	e-Chapter 11 – God's Eternal Character	$9.95
17	ECH-12	e-Chapter 12 – The False Salvation Doctrine	$9.95
18	ECH-13	e-Chapter 13 – A Light On My Path	$9.95
19	ECH-14	e-Chapter 14 – The Gift of Jesus	$9.95
20	ECH-15	e-Chapter 15 – Myth - God Heals Everyone	$12.95
21	ECH-16	e-Chapter 16 – Myth - God Owns Solid Rock	$12.95
22	ECH-17	e-Chapter 17 – Myth - Giving 10% Is A Tithe	$12.95
23	ECH-18	e-Chapter 18 – Myth - Abortion Doesn't Matter	$12.95
24	ECH-19	e-Chapter 19 – Myth - Sexuality Doesn't Matter	$19.95

Continued

| 25 | ECH-20 | e-Chapter 20 – Myth - Politics Doesn't Matter | $12.95 |
| 26 | ECH-21 | e-Chapter 21 – Myth - Everybody Gets To Go | $12.95 |

Instructions: Order online at http://www.bookofedward.org. When ordering by fax or mail, include all information below and provide credit card signature to authorize charge. *Calculate the total of your order and Add 6.875% Sales Tax if you are in MN. Also add $15.00 to cover shipping and handling. Fax Orders to (763) 441-7174 or Mail Orders to Apostle Ministry, Inc., 18140 Zane Street NW #410, Elk River, MN 55330.

Payment Method

Credit Card: Discover____Visa____MasterCard____Amex____
My Check Is Enclosed____

Card Name: _____

Card No: _____

Card Expires: _____ Card Security Code: _____

Email: _____

Ship Name: _____

Address: _____

City: _____ State: _____ Zip: _____

Phone: _____ Fax _____

Cell/Mobile Phone _____

Date: _____

Signature: _____

Other Books
Mail & Fax Order Form

#	ISBN	Description	Price
27	978-0-9768833-6-4	Trinity Dogma	$27.95
28	978-0-9768833-7-1	Seven End-Times Messages From God	$27.95

Follow instructions on prior page and specify quantity desired.

Copyright Notice

Thank you for purchasing "Seven End-Times Messages From God." Copyright laws protect this written work of Reverend Edward G. Palmer. Distribution to others in any form is a violation of copyright laws. Volume discounts are available. Contact the author for further details. Thank you for respecting copyright laws. God will bless your honesty. This work is a ministry to Christians with God's message that they need to love HIS Word more than they love the doctrines of their Church.

Copyright 2009
Rev. Edward G. Palmer
All Rights Reserved